*Turn Right At The Rainbow:
A Diary of Househunting, Happenstance
& Home*

ISBN 978-1-909905-86-3
Copyright © Roz Morris 2026

All rights reserved. No part of this book may be reproduced or transmitted in any form or by any means, graphic, electronic or mechanical, including photocopying, recording in audio or video form, taping or by any information storage or retrieval system, without the express, written permission of the author. This permission must be granted beforehand. This includes any and all reproductions intended for non-commercial or non-profit use.

rozmorris.wordpress.com

Author's note: the events described in this book are real. Certain characters have fictitious names and identifying characteristics.

Published by
Spark Furnace, Cambridge House CB10

Cover art by Leo Hartas
and Roz Morris

ROZ MORRIS

TURN RIGHT AT THE RAINBOW

*A diary of
Housebunting
Happenstance
&
Home*

Contents

Location, Location

Guessing Games *12*

Unexpectedly, This Became Home *16*

We Know Nothing About Moving House *24*

Not Quite Londoners *26*

Stopped World *32*

Not Like You Think It Will Be *35*

Contents

Let the Right One in

A Portrait In The Attic *38*

We Are Too Unusual *40*

Looking

We've Got This *48*

Here You Are At Home *54*

House Viewing: The Romcom Rules *56*

Bad Dates *64*

Rusty Tractor *68*

Sound Check *71*

Beginning A London Life *73*

Unexpectedly Reavailable *81*

Romcom Rules: The Fallback House *83*

Contents

Stuff and Nonsense

A Voyage Through Junk *88*

Try Not To Have A Piano *92*

Dragon Warriors Ride Again *100*

A Little Book Problem *104*

Before Us. After Us. Without Us

The Old Kingdom *108*

It's Not About You *110*

The Homecoming Surprise *113*

Intruders *115*

Numerology *120*

Reading The Room *121*

A Pilgrimage *124*

Weirdstoned: Under Alderley Edge *131*

Contents

Weirdstoned: Thin Places *141*

Weirdstoned: Your Old Home Is On Reality TV *149*

After Us *156*

The Searchers

The Aardvark House *160*

House Of Hiraeth *169*

Summoned by the Chandeliers Recluse *179*

The Show Must Go On And On *185*

Coming and Going

Where You Belong *190*

Peter Turns The Page *196*

Proving Myself 202

Forever And Adieu *204*

Contents

Still Searching

X-Ray Vision *210*

Romcom Rules: We Can Change *212*

Still Don't Know *214*

Getting Hostile

Aardvark Is Back *218*

Rusty Tractor Is Back *220*

Silly Money *225*

I Have Fallen Out Of Falling In Love *229*

The Stone Tape *234*

In Which We Save Calvin From Himself *237*

Turn Right At The Rainbow *240*

Happenstance *242*

Contents

It's Happening

The Chain Is Humming *252*

Gone But Not Forgotten *255*

We Are Its First *257*

Auld Acquaintance *260*

The Snagging Survey *262*

What Vera And Calvin Did Next *269*

The Dust Is Settling *279*

Location, Location

Guessing Games

Home. The root of your routines, the origin of your adventures, the end of your explorations, the protector of your most private times.

You know home like your own limbs, its mirrors and light switches and doorways. If you change their positions, you can't unlearn where they used to be. If you leave, you forever go back in your dreams.

And home begins as a place you've never before been to.

Dave and I are househunting. Each time we walk through a new gate, it could be The One. But will we know?

Guessing Games

How will we know?

At the house we are viewing now, we have doubts. There is a front garden with a strip of lawn and smartly trimmed hedges as straight as walls. We're not gardeners and this will take endless upkeep. We've never even pushed a lawnmower. And this is just the front? What mowing, pruning and weeding duties wait at the back? Is this the right house for us?

Every detail is a question.

Inside, the hallway is dark. Can we fix that with paint? Leave a door always open? The rooms are a good size but the vibe is uncomfortably ersatz. That might be the fake gilded door handles and window-catches, which we're hyper-noticing because they are not us. If we change them, will this house feel right?

We can't know. We have to guess.

I announce the news in our Christmas cards. 'Big change! Our house is on the market. We hope to move out of London next year.' The reaction is surprise, disbelief. But you've been there for x years, where x is thirty for me and thirty-eight for Dave.

Most of our crowd left London long ago, following jobs, loves, family imperatives and itchy feet. We have remained here. We are writers. We keep our dramas and upheavals for our books, or we try to.

Our wandering friends visit from time to time. They have new professions, new life missions, new achievements, new PhDs, new partners, new offspring, new in-laws, new surnames, new survivals. They find us under the same roof (almost; the roof has been refurbished) and behind the same front door (now a smarter colour). Your house never changes, they say.

They endure a night on our sofabed and that also hasn't changed. We apologise for their creaking stoop next morning. We don't know what the sofabed is like to sleep on. We realise the sofabed is thirty-five years old, and they probably slept on it when it was new.

We should replace it. When we visit them they have proper guest bedrooms. We will have a guest room too, in the new house. But there's no sense in buying more furniture yet. We'll have to move it and we're already stuffed with stuff.

Stuff is significant. There are books and podcasts about stuff. *A History Of The World In 100 Objects*. *Shakespeare In 100 Objects*. The quiet everyday things that witness how we live. Home is the ultimate of these.

This house of ours, of thirty and thirty-eight years, is a home and a home country.

And now we are looking for its successor.

How do we choose it? We are driving unfamiliar streets, bewildered by first impressions. Does the house feel right? What about its neighbourhood? Can we even guess this now? A petrol station: useful. A bakery with artisan blackboards: encouraging. A school: could be a traffic scrum at certain times of day. Could be screamy.

All this might be our new everyday.

'At the roundabout, take the tit.'

Our satnav sometimes swallows a syllable. That

'tit' was 'exit', first or second, but which? It also has too many details to process.

We take, it seems, the correct tit.

We are standing in a house with a demanding garden, troubling door handles and doubtful amounts of light. Which of these details will matter and which might we cease to notice? If this becomes ours it will simply be itself.

Is this The One?

Unexpectedly, This Became Home

This house became my home unexpectedly.

The first time the house saw me, thirty years ago, I wasn't a prospective owner.

I lived on the opposite side of London, with a steady boyfriend, with no plans to change either of those things.

I was here to meet a friend of a friend, to travel to a laser-tag game.

I was late. Thanks to a dumb mistake with directions, because I didn't know the area, I went to the wrong station and finally arrived to find a very quiet house because the laser-tag party had left.

Was it even the right house? Nobody rushed out and cried 'you're just in time', so I wasn't sure. It seemed not to have a number. Flustered and rehearsing my excuses, I did not see the number was on a small enamel plate on the gatepost, and also on the front door, weathering into the wood.

In the movie of this essay, that confusion would thrum with metaphor. Look, everybody. She doesn't know where she is.

It was Dave's house.

The house sat in the November sunshine, keeping its own counsel. It had characterful stripy beams and pretty diamond-pane leaded lights. Dismissive folk would describe it as mock Tudor. Those who like that would say Arts and Crafts.

I liked it.

The house was quiet, so I did what everyone does in this situation. Rang the bell, listened, heard nothing. Repeated so the house could relent, reset and send a person out.

It did not. I went home.

Bless, the movie viewer would say. She has no idea what's in store for her and this house.

My goof was forgiven and I returned a few times for parties. I met people who were exciting and exotic. They were artists and writers. I was in awe. My own friends were in graduate corporate careers, in software, or the law, or banking. I worked on a magazine but it was also corporate, for the construction industry. But the people who came to Dave's house were a breed I'd never encountered. They made books that were read for fun and enjoyment, when people were not at work, when they were being their real selves.

In the summer, I was told, friends would stand in the church pulpit in the back garden to read out stories they'd written.

'The back garden has a church pulpit?' I said. I peered into the November darkness. All I could see was skinny weeds and a thicket of dead brambles.

'You'll have to come back in summer and read out a story,' said somebody. I can't remember who that was, though I must now know them very well. I do remember thinking I wouldn't dare read a story to these people who lived by their talents in writing and art. While wishing, very dearly, that I could.

Then a few months later I was arriving in a big way. Not with a story. With a packed bag and a trail of chaos behind me. To move in with Dave. Bewildered and uncertain as on that first afternoon, and now on a cosmically different scale.

Unexpectedly I was changing my life.

I had been with the steady boyfriend for six and a half years. Now I was tearing that up. How long had I known Dave? Not even six months. I'd met him five months before, talked to him a few times, and known him properly for one whole week.

I am not an adventurous person, which is why I write memoirs about unadventures because they're plenty for me. This was not my usual behaviour.

Friends asked for explanations. I had none. I just did it.

The night I moved in, I gazed out into the darkened garden. 'Where's the famous pulpit?' I still hadn't seen it.

'It's out there under that clump of ivy,' said Dave. 'Are you any good at gardening?'

'Terrible. But I love that you've got a pulpit in your garden.'

'Your garden,' said Dave. 'Now you can say you've got a pulpit in your garden.'

My garden? Did it feel like my garden and my house? This turn of events seemed profoundly right but also profoundly reckless.

Perhaps it's something that happens in your mid-twenties. Several of Dave's friends had, without warning, broken long-term relationships and found the sudden and right love of their life. One of my own friends at work did too, shortly after I did. She left her boyfriend of seven solid years to move in with a guy she hardly knew. 'I've done a Roz,' she said, shocked at herself.

I was also shocked at myself.

The house kept reminding me. Roz, did you think about this properly?

It was always full of visitors, who were more at home than I was. Writers and artists working with Dave on books or games. Groups arriving for weekly roleplaying games or friends staying for the weekend. They marched in as they had done for years, with ciabatta and Stilton from the deli, and went to the kitchen to fix a sandwich, a bit surprised to be introduced to me. They knew where to find plates and knives and pickle and where to stash the beers. I didn't yet know what was in all the cupboards. Some regularly stayed overnight and kept a toothbrush here. They'll never know how overwhelming this was to me, their easy use of the house and its stuff and, also, obviously, their long familiarity with Dave. I felt like I was the visitor.

My own friends were just as disorientated. They took me for serious talks, said this was not like me, wanted to make sure I was sure. Some of them gave Dave the serious talk.

Was I sure? Of course I was sure. I offered evidence. I was changing my address on numerous documents. There's a lot of admin when you elope in chaos. I was extracting myself from the mortgage with my ex-boyfriend, paying him compensation because he was in negative equity. Didn't that say I was sure?

The house kept asking. Is this where you should be? Do you feel settled? When the visitors weren't here, it kept their ghosts as well as their toothbrushes. I had the strongest feeling that another person was living here too, moving between the rooms just out of sight.

I'd arrived with no furniture. I let my former boyfriend keep it. Anyway, this house had everything because Dave's mother had an active network of neighbours with stuff they needed to offload. There were wooden chairs galore, with yellowed varnish. There were two dining tables, one of which lived upstairs for board games. There was much 1970s brown and orange. I was borrowing the house from an earlier time.

My colleague who 'did a Roz' went back to her original boyfriend. Her life-changing romance wasn't for ever, as it turned out. Knew it couldn't last, said various people, with scrutinising looks at me. But Dave's friends who'd made spur-of-the-moment marriages were happy and thriving. Who were we more like?

Could I stop being weird and worried?

I didn't find a padlocked den of Bluebeard secrets. But among the house's ghosts I found relics from Dave's first fiancée. I was second fiancée. They'd split several years before and she was now married, but she'd moved out piecemeal, and not entirely. There was a wooden chest in the hall that belonged to her. There were wall hangings and wineglasses.

We sent them back to her via her brother, who was another regular guest. He reported that she wasn't grateful. 'That woman's in my house,' she grumbled. I never met her or saw pictures of her, but I had a feeling that she was still here, like all the other people, and also because some of the things she left behind were garments. A tiny satin skirt on a wardrobe shelf. Itsy lace underwear in the airing cupboard. These were sassy shoes to fill. Was I exciting enough?

The second Mrs de Winter might understand the feeling.

Could I just stop being so fretful? There were no secrets to fear. Dave and I were having a great time.

And first fiancée now lived in Switzerland, where she was contentedly raising a family.

We took control of the house. Much of the downstairs décor was chosen by the first Mrs de Winter. Vinyl moiré wallpaper; crimson paint above the picture rail. I detested the wallpaper but appreciated the crimson. I'd always wanted a house in tempestuous colours. We painted the lounge bordello red, the dining room forest green with gold on the woodwork. Some of the décor was left by the owners before Dave. Graphic designers with kooky tastes, they had painted blue water patterns on the upstairs doors and landing, like an aquarium.

'What are you going to do about the whacky doors?' chuckled one of Dave's friends, as if he hoped my tastes would be sensible.

'Keeping them,' I said. 'I love the doors.'

We painted Dave's office Egyptian blue to match the Arts and Crafts fireplace and put a giant gold Eye of Horus across the entire width of the chimney breast.

Now we have lived in this house for more than half our lives. We've extended and made it more grown up, which meant goodbye gold and red and green, and goodbye water patterns, and goodbye Eye of Horus. But don't be fooled. The chairs and tables from Dave's mother's neighbours are still here, sanded and painted. The gaming dining table is in my office, painted lilac with black legs, sitting under my computer as I type, under every book I've written.

The pulpit in the garden died. During a

thunderstorm, I looked out of the kitchen window and saw it, split open on the crazy paving like a flatpack. Maybe it rotted with age. Maybe it took offence at our recent fancy dress party, where people came dressed as members of the spirit world. (Stranger things have happened here. In October 1987 the guys cast a storm spell in a roleplaying game and awoke to the country's worst hurricane.) I howled when I saw the pulpit in pieces. I seized a chisel and went out in the deluge, rescued the panels and put them in the loft.

Now we are trying to sell this house. Crikey. But the pulpit, our legendary pulpit, will come with us.

We Know Nothing About Moving House

This is not a book of statistics, of how many people move house every year, of how many deals go through or fall through.

This is not a book of tips or typicals. Real life has no typicals.

This is not a book of advice. We are the least suitable people to give advice. In househunting there seems to be a game to play, and we are playing it without reading advice and with little prior experience. Surely it's simple. Get an offer, find a house we like for that price, buy it?

Surely all we need is instincts, honesty and common sense?

Tip from the future: these assumptions will, at times, make people furious with us. We will find we are not good examples of how to behave when buying and selling a house. You should not do what we do.

Our housemoving experience is tiny. Here's mine. I was born in the north of England. From age two I was in the same house until I left for college, age eighteen, when I went 200 miles south to London, and I have been in London ever since. University halls of residence, then a flat share, then a first flat, then I met Dave.

Dave's moving history is also short. He grew up in Surrey, in a house his parents bought when he was very young. Then came university in Oxford and some nomad years, then a rental or two in London, then he made his one and only property purchase, this house, a bit run down. He had friends as lodgers in the early years, they migrated away, as did first fiancée, then I came along.

We're settlers, not movers.

But gradually we have realised we might belong somewhere else.

Not Quite Londoners

I came to live in London aged eighteen. I yearned for an arty career. I wasn't sure which of the arts I wanted to do, but London seemed to hold all the possibilities.

I wasn't sure how I'd make this career. I had no examples in my family. My father was a sales rep for big pharma. My mother ran businesses.

School was little help. I wasn't one of the stars in drama or music or art. I wasn't a star in anything. I wasn't friends with the kids whose families were in theatre or TV, who I envied because they were surely set for interesting futures. I was just quiet.

But I lived loudly in my imagination, in books, music, TV, films, art. In those, I followed the strange, found where I belonged and who I belonged with, fulfilled my destiny, owned ponies and rode them bravely. (This last was important to Kid Roz.)

Every weekend, my parents took *The Sunday Times*. The colour supplement ran interviews with actors, writers, directors, composers and musicians. I read them with fierce longing. These people made the things that mattered most to me. I wanted to do that.

I didn't tell anyone my secret ambitions. I didn't dare. In a small school in a village in the north of England, I didn't think such a life was in my reach. I hadn't been chosen for it — by the school or by the people who were already in those worlds. If I confessed my hopes I would be mocked and misunderstood. 'You want your picture in the Sunday papers, Roz? You want to be famous?'

That wasn't it at all, the fame. It was those lives so full of good purpose.

A plan was taking shape in my mind, without me realising. These artists, I noticed, all lived in London. They were photographed walking thoughtfully along a path by the Thames, or working at desks or pianos in townhouses, from where, at any moment, they could hop on a Tube train to a studio or a theatre or a place where they were needed for their special thing.

That, I decided, was the key. London. It could happen there. It would never happen 200 miles away in the north, among the Muggles. But just by walking around the centre of London, you could brush past places where greatness was in progress. Drama and music schools, art academies, galleries, theatres, music venues, branches of the BBC, the offices of newspapers, book publishers and literary agents. London's places were known throughout the land and far beyond. Foyles bookshop. Buckingham Palace. The streets on the Monopoly board. Mornington Crescent.

And so I would go to London.

Then what? I had no clue. I wasn't like the bold go-getters in *The Sunday Times*. I could never hustle my way into a job in TV or theatre or get a break by dazzling a stranger in an interesting place. When I go to an interesting place I don't find it easy to talk to people. I want to drift with a camera or notebook.

But I got myself to London, because if I didn't I wasn't trying hard enough.

I went to galleries and gigs and museums, but I found I preferred my explorations to be self-curated, in second-hand record shops, vintage emporia, antique markets, junk shops, learning what interested me, letting things speak to me on their own terms, searching for wonder. One day I needed to visit the family records office in Chancery Lane for a copy of a wedding certificate and I stayed for hours. I discovered I could look up anything I liked, the births, marriages and deaths of anyone I knew or used to know, then anyone whose dates I could remember, even rock stars, even the Queen. I didn't have a use for this information, just a joy in finding how complete it was, all together in one floor of an old building in this city, in ruled ledgers.

The whole world was available in London, whatever world you chose to seek.

In this way, by following lights under unexpected doors, I found my own London as a writer, the London I hoped for. Now, when I get on the Tube it might be to travel to publishers, literary agents or events that need my special thing. No one takes my picture for Sunday papers but that has never been the aim. The aim is to be part of the noble engine of creation, the life of the inventive mind, and to make things.

Dave has ended up in London a bit less deliberately. By the time I meet him he is tired of it, regardless of what Samuel Johnson might think. London is convenient for the necessaries of author life but Dave prefers Surrey, a short train ride away, where he grew up, with its heaths and woods. He goes there regularly to escape from streets.

I don't feel the need to escape from streets. Or do I? I find, little by little, I do.

It begins when I notice a girl in a supermarket who is wearing riding boots. These are not fashion boots. On the inner edge are pale marks from the horse's coat. I am suddenly Kid Roz again, remembering my utter devotion to horse books, how I helped neighbours with their ponies, occasionally getting a ride, proud to have the white bloom on my boots afterwards. The marks that proved I had been riding.

After this supermarket encounter, my horse life

starts. 'London is the best city for learning to ride,' I am told. Of course it is. London is best for everything you want to do. It's like Harrods. I take a riding lesson once a week in an indoor school in Dulwich. Soon I am riding in more adventurous places. A heath in Kent. Wimbledon Common. Richmond Park. Riding twice, three times a week, more if I can. I find a yard in Surrey, with deeper woods, bigger heaths, long miles through rain, snow, sunshine, the emerald abundance of spring, the orange opera of autumn.

Dave likes this horsey territory I have found. He comes for walks while I ride. We fit our lives around it, visiting the countryside most mornings, working into the night, which suits many of the people we write and edit with as they're in the US. We become natives of the village near the stables, using its butchers and grocers. We're on 'hi-how-are-you' terms with people in the shops, the cafes, the MOT garage and the gym. Then we get in the car and drive for an hour back to our house in London for work and sleep.

Friends say: 'You're mad. You need to move.'

We view a few houses for sale but moving seems too difficult. To sell our house we'd have to tidy, make our offices look like bedrooms, all unthinkable because there's proper work to do.

My father dies and I am yanked into bitter squabbles with his friends and neighbours. I feel I will never again be carefree. I go for a ride. The horse's sure walk, enjoying a hill on long reins, seems so uncomplicated. Just me and this creature in the woods in a trusting stride. The turmoil is gone. I am blessed to have this.

And then it is March 2020.

The rules are issued. Stay in your homes. Go out for shopping or one hour of exercise locally per day. Don't travel.

We are locked down. In the city.

Stopped World

There's a book called *Househunting*, by the American photographer Todd Hido. He has captured the outsides of ordinary houses at dusk and night, the windows glowing blue from a TV or yellow from a lamp or ceiling light, some through curtains or shutters, some showing the room in full clarity like a set for a stage play. Hido juxtaposes them with the interiors of empty homes, bare rooms with the scars of departures, outlines on the walls of removed furniture and pictures. Presence and vanished presence.

Seen together in this way, the lighted houses are mysterious and warming, each one a private kingdom, declaring its life to the evening. In the pandemic lockdown, the houses have never been so full, all at once, all hours of the day and night.

Dave and I are well, and grateful for that. Grateful also that isolation is our usual work mode and that our work continues. We are already good at making our own working day. And online, everyone is still out and about.

In real London, they are not.

There is no traffic. Our house is near to a school. Usually our road is a swarm of chattering children and parents, at 8.30am and 3.30pm, and mid morning when the kids are walked en crocodile to the common for sports.

Now you can hear a hammer drop several gardens away. If a burglar alarm starts up, it never wails for more than a few seconds. There are people here, more of them than ever, but the street has taken a vow of stillness, as if everyone is sitting an exam.

Suddenly, one evening, people on our street open doors, show themselves and start to applaud. Standing in lighted hallways, whistling, cheering. I find this so touching.

I write about it on Facebook. 'Wow, this spontaneous thing happened, and we all decided to show each other we're not alone.'

'But Roz,' comes the reply. 'It was Clap for the NHS. It's been everywhere, all over social media, the news. How did you miss it?'

Yes, how? These last few days I've seen news galore

but there's so much news, all the time. The clapping event is everywhere, but each of us has our own everywhere.

And this is the problem. Our everywhere has gone badly wrong. We are surrounded by city, grids of built-up streets and skies of roofs and chimneys and phone masts and tower blocks. But that's not where we live.

When the lockdowns end, many people emerge with life-changing epiphanies. This is ours. Our two-part life is absurd. For the time it takes, the petrol it takes, the money, the carbon footprint and the freedom that we have learned is fragile.

Not Like You Think It Will Be

My friend Karen is moving from London to a village 300 miles away in Cumbria.

After weeks of packing and preparations, it is moving day. Once the lorry has driven away, she loads the last things into the car and sends an email.

'I feel just awful. Shell shocked. We lived there for twenty-five years and now it's not ours any more. I suppose I will gradually learn to feel at home in the new house but I feel we have abandoned it unloved to strangers, leaving it lost and empty.'

She's sent this as a warning to me. 'You might go through a similar rollercoaster when you leave your house. You start out feeling callous and cynical, wondering how much it will fetch, and end up weeping and hugging the walls saying sorry we sold you.'

She knows me well. I'm silly about items of long acquaintance. Cars, for instance. I keep them until they die. My first was scrapped because the gearbox seized. My second because a shunt from a fire brigade vehicle did expensive damage to the fuel system. The day the tow-truck arrived, Dave and I watched in grave silence while hoists were fastened around its front axles and it was dragged away, after all the miles it did for us.

I talked to another friend about this. He knew the feeling. 'I've always left a talisman in the car,' he said, 'to help it on its way.'

How will I feel about the house? I've no idea. What will it be like to lock the door and leave it empty?

Karen's right. These are days of purpose and innocence. We're thinking only of our immediate goal, impressing the estate agents. Though they can buzz off if they suggest we put our desks in storage and replace them with beds 'so people can see your offices are actually bedrooms'.

But it's time to pimp the house and say 'buy me'.

Let The Right One In

A Portrait In The Attic

We've appointed an estate agent. We've studied Rightmove to learn how houses should be presented. Most have a statement clock on the wall, like a railway station. Or a statement guitar. Family portraits also seem to be fashionable, to suggest a fondly regarded place with good memories.

We have a portrait. But we are keeping it hidden. It's not very good.

It's a big photographic print, a gift from our wedding photographer. It's not a studio portrait. There's no carefully tuned lighting to find our good angles and create a sense of glamour or occasion.

A Portrait In The Attic

It's a snapshot of two grinning people taken with a flash against grey hotel curtains. We married in a hotel room in Mexico City with no wedding trappings. Just us, a judge and some highly excited witnesses borrowed from the back office. The photographer was somebody's friend who put on a bow-tie and brought a camera. We loved the pictures, but they're not the kind you enlarge, especially not to poster size.

What to do with this portrait? This has always been a problem. It's too naff to put on a wall, too significant to throw away. For years, it has been kept behind boxes of printer paper. Before that it was adopted by Dave's mother, because she was afraid we'd bin it, but we noticed she kept it inside a wardrobe.

Now that our house has to look like a show home, it's been put away in the roof, where clutter is acceptable. I guess you could say we now have a portrait in the attic.

We've boxed up a heap of books, including books we've written ourselves, and the paper mountains from our offices, because buyers don't want to see those.

While buyers look around, discussing how they'll stamp themselves on each space, the attic is bursting with our happy creative clutter. It also has our photo albums. Old saddles from horses past and present. My current horse's summer wardrobe. Hats I've worn to weddings. These items are the house's true personality, its heart and history.

The portrait, from our very first year here together, stands watch.

We Are Too Unusual

There is feedback from the viewings. It is maddening and absurd.

A few buyers say the layout of the house won't work for them. If feedback is supposed to help you improve or understand something, I struggle to see what we do with this information. The layout is the layout.

Also, is the layout not visible on the floorplan? Why did these people even come?

And the layout is not outlandish. While we've been window-shopping on Rightmove we've seen houses with bedrooms downstairs and rooms that have no windows. That's outlandish. Our house has everything where you'd expect to find it. Also, our roof is new and we've repainted inside and out. Shouldn't that make us desirable?

'Your house is unusual,' says Calvin, our estate agent. 'People in this area want the Victorian terraces and semis, which all look the same inside. Two rooms on each floor, stairs up the side wall. Your house is, er, different.'

These buyers should have seen our era of gold picture rails and painted water patterns. And the giant Eye of Horus in Dave's office, I mean the second bedroom.

Calvin also tells us our house has too few bathrooms. We cannot see the problem. Plumbers are plentiful. Notice how much building work goes on in these streets. To add another bathroom, just open the front door and whistle.

One prospective buyer says there are too many stairs. Again, behold the floorplan. Also the estate agent's pictures and video. They were in plain view, these sneaky stairs, before the buyer came. So why did they come?

Another sore point is the EPC rating, the score for our house's energy efficiency. Most modern houses are C or B. Calvin sends a surveyor who looks around and tells us our score is E, which is as bad as it sounds.

We question the surveyor. 'Seriously? E? The house is double glazed except for a couple of windows on the stairs. It is fully insulated in the roof.'

'I can't check the roof insulation,' says the surveyor.

We take him up the stairs again to the top floor, open a storage cupboard in the roof space and show him the thermal panels fitted into the rafters. 'This is throughout the entire roof,' we explain. 'We replaced all the tiles and added insulation.'

'I have to see the insulation in my inspection,' says the inspector.

'Well as you can see, the top-floor bedroom is built into the roof so the insulation is part of the ceiling. You can inspect it if you drill a hole from the attic next to the bedroom and put a camera through.'

'I don't have a drill or a camera.'

Indeed, he doesn't have any instruments. Just a notebook and his phone. He doesn't even take pictures. Is this normal?

'We can show you receipts for replacing and insulating the entire roof.'

'But I have to see the insulation,' says the surveyor. 'It might not be all over.'

'You could see it if you use a drill and a camera.'

Silence. We wonder what kind of surveying school he went to.

We try another approach. 'Think about it. Why would we insulate a cupboard, which we don't spend any time in, but not the bedroom, which we are in for the whole night?'

'If I can't see the insulation,' says the surveyor, and writes 'E' in his notebook.

After he's gone, Dave finds photos of the roof works.

They show the stripped timbers with the insulation going on. We send them to the surveyor, who says 'That isn't proof the whole roof was done', and files his verdict on the government website.

Calvin says: 'Ah, don't worry about that E rating. Nobody will notice.'

Won't they? We wouldn't view any house with an EPC of E.

We establish a routine when buyers come round. We leave the house, hide in the car and try to identify who's coming to our door. Is it that guy, who's checking the road name and has stopped for a long think? I am cheered if I see bohemian clothes. Definitely excited when a woman arrives on a Vespa, removes her helmet, shakes out a peppy haircut, climbs off and straightens her skirt. She has cool hair and she rides a Vespa in a skirt and skinny boots. I think she'll like the house.

She's not a buyer, says Calvin later. She's a scout for a buyer.

That's a thing? People can afford to pay an assistant to do their househunting? We are in an alien world.

Despite all these viewings, and criticisms whose purpose we cannot decipher, there are no offers.

'Try lowering the price,' says Calvin.

'But that was the price you advised.'

'It's always tricky to know what a house will get if it's not like all the others.'

We lower the price.

'Now you've lowered the price,' says Calvin, 'you

might get a few bids so you'll end up with more money in the end.'

There are no bids.

We settle into not-selling. The viewings taper off but any moment we might have to spruce the house back to viewing condition. Like the fire brigade, we develop an emergency routine. Throws and cushions in strategic positions, especially to cover the sag in the sofabed. The buyers aren't here for the sofabed, but we've learned they might condemn the whole house for it. Remember, they can't see stairs on a floorplan.

As we tiptoe in from another wait in the car, shivering in the February darkness, we meet today's couple. The guy is wearing shorts despite the cold. 'It needs work,' he says, 'but every house does.' He sounds cheerful.

Could he be the one?

'He was thinking about an offer,' says Calvin the next day, 'but his own buyer just pulled out.'

Back to not-selling.

Then a second viewing. Our first second viewing. It's the Grinning Shorts Couple. A few days later, there's an offer. It's substantially lower than the already-lowered asking price. If the house price is a human figure, our reduction lopped off both feet. Now it has lost a whole leg as well.

But Calvin couldn't be happier. They're cash buyers, he says. 'They've moved out of their house and are renting. It's a strong position.'

'It's not enough,' we say, 'to buy another house.'

Calvin is undaunted. 'Shall we say you'll meet them half way?'

'No, because they'll take that as the new asking price and carry on downwards. The offer is not enough.'

'I think these are your buyers,' says Calvin. 'We've shown the house to so many people and nobody else has made an offer. Your house is difficult. And you had that low EPC rating.'

Eventually the Grinning Shorts Couple offer more. Now we've got half the leg back, which is better. But are we letting it go too cheaply?

There's only one way to know.

Dave makes the call to Calvin. 'Okay, we accept that offer if we can find a house we like for that price.'

As he is speaking, there is a sudden cascading clatter in the wall, of mortar coming loose inside the chimney. Sometimes this happens because the chimneys are old, but this is the loudest noise we've ever heard from it. As if the house is displeased.

Looking

Looking

We've Got This

I confess there's a game I play when I'm in another person's house. What would I change if I lived there? Repaint that wall? Remove the wall entirely? Apologies, friends. I assume you do it too.

Now, Dave and I are doing this, both of us, and it's not a game.

It's a one-time decision too, because we'll have to pay stamp duty on the house we buy, which is a tax on the purchase price, a much, much bigger expense than legal and moving fees. It adds another leg to the cost of the house. We can't afford to get this wrong.

How to know if a house is right for us? It might seem blissfully peaceful while we're visiting on a weekday at 1pm, but what about other times of day and night? Should we sneak back on a Sunday afternoon when the community alphorn orchestra is in session?

We see a house we like. It's 1930s like ours, close to where Dave grew up. It feels like we already know it. The EPC is good. There are things we'd change, of course. Why so many fitted wardrobes? Which ones shall we tear out? We look at perfectly good cupboards, considering vandalism.

Its showstopper is an extended lounge at the back with rooflights. It's the kind of space you want to laze in, basking in the sunshine, or lying back and looking at the rain. We realise one of our must-haves: a room with light from above. This becomes a phrase we repeat often. It sounds religious. We'd like a house with light from above.

The house also has an attic room. Our current house has that. A den in the roof. We like it.

We see the house on an open day. An open day is an event where the estate agent crowds in as many viewings as possible, close together, so the people leaving see more people arriving and everyone gets in a panic. We are certainly panicking about this house. The other viewers will surely be bidding.

We tell ourselves: don't fall in love with a place until everything is certain.

We have a few other houses to see that day. One is

still under construction. We're interested because it will have workmanship guarantees. Our own house is eighty-three years old and when it needs repairs, Dave swears it's a constant hassle and we should sell it. He would love a house built to modern standards. I would love a house that doesn't exasperate him. But this house is too unfinished to judge. Every room is the ruddy brown of drying plaster so we can't tell if it will be light or dark. The kitchen and bathrooms aren't yet fitted. We peer into the crates of cabinets and fittings, trying to envisage the spaces when everything is installed and painted. Will they be big or cramped?

We see a house converted from a Victorian inn on the edge of a heath. I have known this building for decades. Back then, it was an abandoned hulk with curved brickwork and latticed windows into black cobwebbed spaces. A bikers' nightclub once upon a time, locals told me. I'd love it as my house, I thought, as is my habit with any characterful place that has fallen derelict. Now it has been converted by a developer and we can consider it for real.

The inn is indeed an impressive house. The main room, which was the bar, is open to the rafters. There's enough space above the kitchen and lounge for a trapeze act. Spiral staircases ascend to smaller sitting areas on balconies over the main chamber. But the bedrooms are on the floor below, and dark as a Goth's dreams. Good for sleeping, terrible for working, which is how we'd use them. We'd spend all day with the electric light on, which we both hate. The inn is a stylish pad, but not practical for us.

Its estate agent phones as we drive away. There's an offer and we're only just out of the door. We don't regret losing it, but things move worryingly fast. We'd better pounce on the 1930s house.

We call the estate agent.

Apparently we're too early to make an offer.

Too early to make an offer? Who made that rule? Don't they want to sell this house?

The bids will be gathered in a few days' time, we're told. Meanwhile, we should come for a second viewing.

So we can't offer right now and get an answer?

No.

On the second visit, the estate agent starts the hard sell.

'This house has marvellous proximity to schools.'

We are delighted to parry: 'We don't need schools. No children.'

'It's handy for the station.'

'We're not commuters.'

But the estate agent knows his craft. He tries again. 'We've had a lot of interest. We're expecting a lot of offers.'

He's got us. We cannot hide the jump of worry in our faces.

He moves in for the kill. 'The house down the road went for a whole leg above the asking price.' He doesn't say 'a whole leg', but it is exactly the amount the Grinning Shorts Couple tried to knock off our house.

Now we are even more disheartened. We have

viewed the house he's talking about. It's a 1980s horror with faux mahogany and an extra lounge accessed through a narrow doorway as though it was once an outhouse. That house will need a lot of work and it's already a whole leg more expensive than this house we're interested in. Now we're hearing it's gone for a further whole leg? (In case you're losing count, take the human figure of our original house price and give it three-and-a-half legs instead of two.)

'It's just mad at the moment,' says the estate agent. He looks happy. Happy at the madness and happy that he's found our tender spot.

Any casual observer would spot how we're being played, but we are completely on the hook. We no longer feel wise.

We drive home. Bugger. Should we offer above the asking price? By how much? This 1930s house is right in so many ways. We don't want to lose it. We've already planned where we'll put everything, which we should not have done, but too late. We'll fit and our stuff will fit. And we have our own offer, and that is a good fit too.

What if prices go up even more? Houses are whirling out of our grasp. Even nasty ones.

We gulp and agree we could go up by half a leg.

We are not in our right minds.

Later that evening, we simmer down. We always vowed we'd avoid a bidding war. That's the road to crazy.

Calvin calls to see how we're doing. He offers

advice. 'The agents are obliged to tell you if there have been other offers. You might find there isn't a bidding war. They want you to think there is.'

Very glad we asked.

The bids are due on Wednesday and the deadline is 5pm. We phone at 4.30. 'Have there been other offers?'

'Not yet, but we're expecting one.'

One offer. That's quite a change from 'lots of interest' and 'madness'.

We phone at 5pm and offer asking price.

'There's one other offer but if you go up a tiny bit it's yours.'

We offer another toe. It's considerably less than the half-leg we thought we'd be offering the day before. In the delirium. In the madness.

We might have got the house. How efficient we are.

And how nearly stupid. Think how close we came to offering over the odds. Indeed, there might be no other offers. We nearly made a big bid against a non-existent army of buyers, when in truth we were bidding against ourselves. Those estate agents know some slippery tricks. We are totally out of our depth.

Next day, the estate agent phones. 'You won the bidding war. But.'

But?

'But the seller has decided not to move after all.'

Looking

Here You Are At Home

Your first home is an accident of birth. Obviously.

Your subsequent homes are also accidents.

You are where you are because somebody else let it go. Even if your home is brand new, someone sold the land it stands on. Their garden. A field. An empty factory. A derelict inn. It's all random. Just what somebody decided at the time.

All this happened because a road was made, perhaps with no buildings on it, only travellers, going beside a field or a wood and not thinking of stopping to live there.

Before that time, before people made it a route, there was only the field or wood. Maybe it was nameless, not a defined place at all.

Come forwards and a time-lapse of that road would show buildings going up, going out sideways, or being split, or coming down and going up on the same ground or growing in the gaps, so the structure and form of your home, which might have made you choose it instead of another one, also come from numerous steps of happenstance, every bit as haphazard as the chances that brought your parents together and made them choose each other, and the chances and genetic shufflings that created them the way they are, and the chances that created you as you are, and the dinosaurs as they were too.

And today, after the accumulation of all these unique and random chances, all these dominoes that suited each other and fell just so, here you are at home.

House Viewing: The Romcom Rules

Househunting follows the rules of a Hollywood romcom. Before you find Mr Right, there are misadventures to have, mistakes to make and lessons to learn. They'll tell you what you're really looking for and what you're not.

This will not be what you thought at the start.

You will meet various stock characters. We have already met the person who plays the field and won't commit. Dave and I learn to ask why a seller wants to move, though this has limited usefulness. We never meet the seller, only the estate agent, and they'll say whatever will please the buyer at that particular moment.

Another of the stock romcom characters is the goofy oddity.

We are shown a house with an astonishing number of loos. There's an ensuite bathroom with loo for every bedroom, and another standalone bathroom with a loo. If everyone's got a bathroom, who is this for? Next to it is another solo loo and downstairs is another solo loo. And beside it, another.

These premises have more accommodation for active bottoms than for whole sleeping people. Was there a peculiar family anxiety? The doors of the two downstairs loos face each other, so the occupants could hold a conversation.

In the romcom, your date might have baggage. The annoying best friend, the high-maintenance ex. In our house odyssey, this is the unwanted annexe. Annexes, we learn, are often grim, but your ideal house might have one and you must take it on. What do you do with an extra mini-house? It depresses you with its décor, which is inferior or dated because the previous owners also didn't want it. It glares at you from its dark windows and never-heated spaces. You're responsible for me too. What do you think about that?

The house for many bottoms has an annexe. It's a dismal set of rooms with institutional colours like a safe house in a movie about the Cold War, where living there is better than being dead, but only just.

'This annexe has been rented out,' says the estate

agent cheerily, 'for £900 a month.'

It was rented? And for £900? This desolate place? Though it does have two loos. The owners have done for others what they'd do for themselves.

Some houses seem chosen for us by fate. We arrive for a viewing on an open day. The estate agent consults her list and reacts with surprise. 'You're Roz and Dave Morris? We found a credit card in the drive with your names on. My colleague has been trying to phone you.'

'Thanks, but that can't be our credit card. We've only just arrived.'

She shows us the card. It does indeed have our names. D and R Morris. Though it is not ours, in romcom rules this is a sign.

In real life, the house is the weirdest so far. It's extended to the very limits — into the roof, out to each side. As if it can't stop growing new rooms. It has eight bedrooms, far more than we need. Do The Waltons live here? Some of the bedrooms are in the attic, and there are fans next to the beds. So there's no insulation in the roof. Even our EPC twit could spot that. The rooms must be ovens in summer, arctic in winter.

The rooms in the side extensions, plural, are freezing cold and long unused. One of them is very peculiar. It has a long window the length of a bus with built-in wooden seating. I count the seats. There are twelve. The seats have lockers underneath. Like a church hall, or a temple, or a scout hut. In a family house. What went on here?

I think about the house with the many loos. Does

each house have a heyday when it lived its bizarre best life?

That night, I dream of a house whose top floor looks onto a roof garden. Instead of plants, it has numerous tiny figures looking back with blinking eyes, like the congregation of a sinister cult.

Another househunting stock character is the well-bred eccentric. We view a 1920s mansion that's been split into several houses. The portion we are viewing has half of the old ballroom. I am ready to be swept off my feet.

But the bisected ballroom doesn't work. It's trying to be the sitting room and it's far too big. A sofa and two armchairs huddle by the fireplace, and the rest of the room is very empty. There's enough space around the furniture to park several cars. Sit by the fire and you'd feel like you were hiding from the rest of the room. The house next door must have got the main ballroom window. This side has a narrow pane at the end. It's dark, which must be why I'm thinking of an underground car park.

But other rooms of the house are so gracious. The staircase is like a stately home. The windows are tall as an abbey. The oak panelling glows golden in the afternoon sunshine. At the back, the lawn has an archway and a set of crescent steps to a lower lawn, then a little bridge into woods. On the wall is a print of the mansion in its original form, proof of its pedigree.

I am charmed, except for that dim downstairs room.

Looking

Could we leave it unused? The other rooms would be enough for our needs. There would be a small sitting room upstairs, a spare room for guests, offices for us.

No, says Dave. Look where that ballroom is. It's in the centre of the house. That would be like having an empty annexe, which you go through every time you walk from the kitchen to the stairs. In winter you'd have to run because it would be perishing cold. And the whole ground floor will always be dark, which will be depressing.

Permanently dark rooms were also the dealbreaker with the Victorian inn.

Old aristocratic houses are beguiling in a brief encounter, a burden as a long-term prospect. They are ruinous to heat. They have leaks that can never fully be fixed. We've already seen one leak in this house and we've only been here twenty minutes. Our own house used to have a persistent and distressing leak from a balcony on the top floor. It brought the ceiling of Dave's office down. We consulted experts, replaced the window, resurfaced the flat roof, enjoyed a few months of relief, then the water torture started again, drip drip drip. No matter what we did it found a way, as if the house contained its own natural spring. Finally one of the drip-whisperers, replacing the window yet again, discovered a hole drilled in a wrong place by a builder long ago, and at last the water sprite dried and went to heaven.

Old houses will suffer from persistent infirmities, bad previous surgeries and bad previous exorcisms.

House Viewing: The Romcom Rules

Farewell, distinguished gentleman with your half-ballroom. Living in you would be exhausting.

So we are now wiser. We have learned what we're not looking for. Nothing period, no matter how beautiful. Nothing with rooms we'll never use. Nothing with zones of perpetual gloom.

When you find a house you like, you open the door to heartbreak. You don't just buy it, like clicking a button on Amazon. You don't just make an offer, like eBay. You can't get confident because your own offer is enough and all the finances work. Remember, there is madness about, and estate agents are doing their special smile as the price grows by a whole leg and maybe an arm as well. You'll be told that others are dating the house, as if you're not good enough. You'll be told they are close to an offer even if they are not. This romcom needs you to feel the agony of unattainability.

In a romcom, your true heart will win. You'll earn the house by proving you deserve it, but in real life the house is not choosing anything.

Every romcom needs a whiff of mortality. Four weddings need a funeral. We look at a probate house. It's in the neighbourhood where Dave grew up in the 1970s. Those were wild days for bathrooms, when white was only for boarding schools. The ensuite has a plum-purple bath, sink and loo, with gold taps. Tiles the colour of asparagus. In the second bathroom the colour scheme is flipped. Asparagus for the porcelain, plum for the tiles. I find myself trying to decide which version I like the best. But sensible people will rip these bathrooms out, and that seems a shame.

In the lounge is a framed letter — a telegram from the Queen for a one-hundredth birthday, reached the previous August. 'I used to walk past this house fifty years ago,' says Dave, 'and this makes me realise the woman who lived here was already fifty then.' We ponder this boggling jigsaw of time. Dave, a teenager, walking by the house and noticing it. 'And now here I am,' he says, 'inside the house, with my wife.'

This house has one of us in its past, and that is a kind of home. We could also be its future. We like its spaces, though the kitchen is tiny and would need an extension, and we might have spirited discussions about whether to keep those bathrooms.

'We've just had an offer,' says the estate agent. 'Above the asking price. And there are likely to be more.'

We can't do a bidding war for this, not with the cost of remodelling. This house will go to a developer, who will demolish any offer we make. Money is the only thing that talks. Not a sense of rightness or the deserving alignment of stories.

'You've got a house on an open day we wanted to see,' we tell the agent, 'just down the road. We asked for an appointment and were told they were full.'

'Let me see what I can do.'

They're not full, and five minutes later we're pulling up outside a 1930s house, which is opposite the 1930s house we won and lost a week ago.

House Viewing: The Romcom Rules

The estate agent greets us with quite aggressive dismay. 'How did you get in to see this?'

We don't say: what's your problem with us, you little snot?

The house gives us good feelings. It looks out on a tranquil tussocky wilderness with a broken-down tractor that has been painted with white emulsion, which is being eaten away by rust. It looks like an artwork.

Its rooms are good. It has a third floor built into the attic, which we like.

The estate agents watch us. They hardly say anything. No jovial patter to rev up our desire. We're not supposed to see this house.

In romcom rules, the last-minute meet is the right one. Especially if you must defy hostile guardians. They don't want you to want it? Start fighting.

We really like the rusty tractor house.

On the shelves in the attic den I spot some of my books, thrillers I ghostwrote several years ago.

My books are already in the house. This is totally a sign.

Bad Dates

'I need to talk to you urgently,' says our solicitor in an email. 'I've just had a call with your estate agent about the contract. You've agreed to move out by September, which is just five months away. And you haven't arranged a house to buy yourselves. I strongly advise you against this.'

We didn't ask anyone to start contracts. What?

'You didn't know any of this?' says our solicitor.

We phone Calvin.

'Your buyers are ready to exchange!' he says. 'Why don't you exchange right now and move into a rental if necessary?'

This wasn't what we agreed. We agreed we would exchange when we found a house we could buy with their offer. Isn't that how it works?

'But Mick and Steph sold and now they're renting,' says Calvin. Mick and Steph are the Grinning Shorts Couple. 'You could agree to a long completion date, of, say, five or six months. September or October.'

No. Because their offer is considerably less than we originally asked and we don't know if it's enough.

'Otherwise you might lose your buyers,' says Calvin. 'I'm having to talk to them every day.'

Now Calvin must be exaggerating. They knew these conditions all along.

Dave says to me: 'He is talking to them every day. He then nags me afterwards. I didn't want to bother you about it.'

Dave composes an email that is diplomatic at world-class level. 'We don't want to lose Mick and Steph. That would be a disaster. But there's only one thing worse, which would be moving out of a house we're happy with to one we're not happy with. So we're very sorry, we can't exchange yet.'

We won't even discuss the suggestion of renting.

All is quiet for a few hours, then Calvin phones. 'Mick and Steph really like your house and will hang on. When they first saw it, they had an offer on their house that they then lost, then they sold it for two legs and an arm more, so they're prepared to wait and rent.'

How spiffing that Mick and Steph did so well from

their sale. Why has Calvin decided to tell us this, with the exact figures too? Surely that's a bit indiscreet.

Afterwards we have much to discuss.

First, we are in the realms of silly money. An offer of two legs and an arm more? (Dear reader, you're right. That's four legs and three arms.) I guess that comforts them while we're dithering.

Second: did they have to beat us down so much?

Third: exactly how does Calvin know how much they sold for? The actual amount? They surely didn't tell him. 'Hey, we could pay a lot more than you think we can...' If you were trying to negotiate a good deal, you'd tell the estate agent your budget was tight.

This is guesswork, but we think Calvin knows because Calvin sold their house.

That suggests a wily set of machinations. Calvin is the agent for Mick and Steph's house. They get a low offer. Accept it, says Calvin. I have a house you can make a cheeky offer on because they've had no takers. Then Mick and Steph lose that sale, get a much higher offer and Calvin says, sell now, move to a rental and I'll get you the Morris house for a song. You're not keen on renting? You won't be renting for long. I'll get the Morrises out. Calvin banks the commission and one of those smiles, Mick and Steph start renting. But the Morrises aren't signing anything until they are sure they can buy another good house, and Mick and Steph are miffed.

'When are they going?' they ask Calvin. 'You said they would.'

So he tells our solicitor we've agreed to move out. Our solicitor, alarmed, tells us 'don't do that'. We say, what's this?

My friend Karen, who warned me about seller's remorse, also told me: 'I hate the way estate agents behave'. I thought she meant their sales language where all roads are highly desirable. The brochure photos where a wide-angle lens has been used to make tiny rooms look big (look for walls that are slanted, corners that look like wedges of cheese, doorways that are stretched and statement clocks like rugby balls). Their deliberate blank looks when you mention this photographic deception at the viewing. The ways they try to panic you. You learn to adjust for all that. But this stunt with the contract?

Our solicitor is astonished. She says: 'I don't normally have an estate agent telling me to do something the seller has never even heard about.'

Rusty Tractor

Here's another thing Karen said: 'It's the estate agents who decide who gets a house.' I thought that made no sense until we got the stink-eye at Rusty Tractor. I swear the agents didn't want us to see it. Why?

Is it promised to another buyer, perhaps to preserve a chain?

We return to the Rusty Tractor house for a second look. Two estate agents are there. Perhaps they'll leave us alone because we're the wrong buyers. Or perhaps they'll close in for the hard sell. We are expecting a discussion about price madness, which we will ignore.

Why are there two estate agents today? I've never seen that before. Have they prepared a double act?

'Dave and I will walk around separately,' I tell them, 'and compare notes afterwards.'

The agents look at each other. That was not the plan. Are they trying to decide who follows Dave and who follows me?

I don't want to be followed. I add: 'We want to look in silence so we can think.'

We look around the house. The agents drift about, declawed. I find their silence amusing.

There comes a moment when we all coincide on the stairs. One of them fishes into his phrase book and says:.

'Houses don't come up in this road very often.'

That's funny. I point across the road to number six. 'We made an offer on that house last month and the owner decided not to sell. And number eleven there —' (I point to another house) '— is about to go on the market and the agent is giving us the first viewing.' (Number eleven never goes on sale, but at the time we are assured it will.)

We're mounting a feisty defence. But what's really lined up for this house? Do we stand a chance?

We decide the Rusty Tractor house is still good. I spot a leak by the ceiling light in the main bedroom, and a problem with another light switch, but they look manageable. We phone and make an offer.

'The seller has put up the asking price by an arm and a leg,' says the agent.

Looking

Has he? That's insane. Or are we the wrong buyers? The home you are in now. Look around. You might be here because you were the best fit for a bigger political plan you knew nothing about.

Sound Check

Our house has a unique song. The tock of its radiators. The hum in the upstairs pipes when a tap is turned downstairs. The tremble of the sliding wardrobe doors in their runners when a big vehicle goes past.

Our house sits in an environment of routine sounds. The rhythm of passing traffic as it changes gear for the hill. The bounce of lorry axles as they hit the dip where, below the surface, one of London's old rivers runs in a pipe. The routine of aircraft above. If we wake in the darkness and the road is quiet and the skies busy, that's around 6am, the rush hour for

Heathrow. If we hear no cars, we wonder if it's Christmas.

Inside its structure and outside in the land, the house tells us we're in a familiar place.

We view a house built into the side of a slate quarry. Part of the garden is vertical. I like that. No weeding or tending, and it creates an appealing, cosy seclusion. But at the end of the road is the railway line. Every fifteen minutes there's a deafening anvil chorus as the inter-city screeches into Guildford.

'How do they cope with that?' I ask the estate agent.

She laughs. 'They tell me they hardly notice it.'

I was curious to see what she'd say.

We view a house that's 1930s, like ours. It has good spaces and big windows. But what's that next door? A community centre with a bowling green and children's playground.

'How noisy is it here?' I ask.

'They tell me they hardly notice it,' laughs the estate agent.

I do my own checks. The community centre is a wedding venue. Fully licensed bar with disco, available for your function until 11pm. I think we'll notice that, and more than hardly.

We're still looking. And listening.

Beginning A London Life

I realise there is only one other time I have househunted on the open market.

I was twenty-one years old, finishing my English literature degree in London, moving out of college halls. I was going to find a place to share with my boyfriend, who was still a student.

My mother was dismayed. She believed my degree in literature was no use for real life. She assumed I would move back up north to the family orbit, to train in something neat and tidy, make that my life forever. Law had been suggested. I'd been 'allowed' to study English in London as a brief fanciful madness.

Looking

I wasn't going back up north. I'd come to London to be in the city where art, TV, music, films and books were made, where people did their own special thing. On the Tube one day I sat opposite a woman who had a live parrot on her shoulder. A green parrot, looking patiently into the distance as she was, swaying with the train, unbothered by stops and starts, and inevitable stares of other passengers. The woman was wearing a jumpsuit of the same green as the parrot. She looked like a scene from a photoshoot or a pop video, but this was her actual day, going about with her parrot, in their team colours. This was London; you could be what you needed to be. I had come to find that.

'London's expensive,' said my mother. 'You won't be able to afford to live there.'

'I'll get a job,' I told her.

I didn't have much time to find the job. Or the place to live. College was letting me rent a room for a week until the start of term, then I had to be out.

First, the job. I didn't know what job. My degree subject didn't equip me directly for modern employment, but English graduates managed to survive somehow. I was good at... what? Reading and thinking. Also cooking. And I had a posh accent, so I got a job in a deli in an expensive part of Fulham.

I thought the job would be the hard part, but then I tried finding a place to live.

With my boyfriend, I looked. We bought the *Evening Standard* as soon as it came off the delivery vans, circled the cheapest rentals and were grateful the student union let us use their phone so we weren't pouring coins into a callbox. Even though we were quick, many had gone by the time we got through. Every student in the city was chasing the same flats.

On the times we won the phone race, the prize was a horror tour of the desolate and depressing.

There was a former hotel in Paddington, a stuccoed building with wedding-cake pillars that were grey and peeling. The flat had been a downstairs reception room. Now it had twin beds, firmly separated by furniture which the landlady said must not be moved. She emphasised this with a prurient narrowing of the eyes that said she'd noticed we were girl and boy and would surely do that sort of thing. Would she come in to check? We asked to see the bathroom. She opened a cupboard in the kitchen. It contained the bath. A bath in a cupboard in the kitchen. When you used it, should you leave the doors open or close them?

There was Notting Hill. Forget the movie with Hugh Grant and Julia Roberts. This wasn't a loft of bonhomie and bedlam behind a boho blue door. It was a basement bedsit, a pit of darkness with a smeared window that was mostly covered with a curtain. I didn't dare lift the curtain to see what was outside. It was the kind of place where people died of broken hearts. Or worse. A year later I read that an entire row of bedsits in the building had been gutted by fire.

Does everyone go through this as a rite of passage? These were places straight from bleak movies of the

1960s, where innocent girls had abortions or were strangled and sealed into the walls.

But they were all I could afford on my shop salary, and my boyfriend was still a student so he was on a shoestring too. My mother was right. I wouldn't be able to afford to live.

While my boyfriend went to lectures, I struck out to the edges of the Tube lines where prices were cheaper. I saw a flat in Acton. The landlord lived below. He was German. He told me there would be a compulsory surcharge for cleaning. His brown pullover was stained and he had his arm in a filthy sling, which suggested he didn't mind dirt at all, but just wanted to inflate the rent.

I sat wearily on the Tube afterwards. This was absurd. I had a job. But in three days I would have no home. My boyfriend could carry on in student halls if necessary, but I had nowhere. I knew no-one in London I could stay with. I thought homelessness did not happen to a person who had a job.

As each day passed, I looked at appalling places and considered, seriously, could I live here? Did the embedded smell of stale oil matter? Here I could begin my London life. The big window straight onto the street which a burglar could open in seconds? Here I could come home to a ransack.

I looked at nicer flats but they were too expensive. Here I could try to live without food. I dreamed of a place that was clean, affordable and sane, that didn't have a bath in a cupboard or the cooker by the bed.

One place seemed to be our salvation: a beamy cottage in Highgate. It was a house share rather than a self-contained flat, so it was in our price range and didn't have the forsaken look of dingy make-do. We'd have a bedroom and would use the kitchen and bathroom alongside the owners. We realised we had to impress the owners, a couple who were the age of our parents. They told us they liked us, especially our zeal for cooking, our polite accents and our appreciation of their Aga. What a relief. The rent was within our budget and the house wasn't frightening.

Or was it? The couple had a cat called Liebling, who shot away at missile speed when the man tried to pick her up. The woman wore a tight black dress and gave my boyfriend several smouldering looks, which was creepy. Remember she was the same age as our mothers. We were running out of time, and we seemed to have a chance here. But that terrified cat, running away in case a hand reached for him, seemed a warning to heed the uncomfortable vibes of the place.

I could live here and be persecuted in ways I couldn't yet guess.

I asked an estate agent in the area for advice. He said: 'We don't handle student rentals because they are too cheap.'

He and I had different definitions of 'cheap'.

'Try Fenella Boxtree up the road,' he said. 'I warn you, she's...' He couldn't find a suitable word to describe Fenella Boxtree.

Fenella Boxtree had a tiny shop the size of a burger

van, completely walled in by filing cabinets. Every time she spoke it sounded like a scolding, as if her insides were a churning furnace of fury. She peered in a folder and brought out a card. 'I have a room in this flat in West Hampstead,' she said, in a tone that said 'you don't deserve it'.

West Hampstead would be a dream. It was close to my old campus, where I'd most like to be. Then I saw the address. 'That one's gone,' I said. 'I phoned when it was in the Standard two days ago.'

'The owner told you that because she didn't like you,' snapped Fenella Boxtree, and picked up the phone.

After a bit of chat, Fenella put the phone down. 'Go and see the room now. But don't be surprised if the landlady doesn't like you.'

Walking to the flat, I thought back to the call a couple of days before.

'Hello, is the flatshare…'

'Sorry, it's taken.'

'Okay, thank you.'

Perhaps I missed something, but I couldn't see how anyone was offended.

The landlady in West Hampstead was friendly and so was the room. It was in an elegant mansion flat. There were no frightening carpets or wallpaper. No chairs that suggested the waiting room of a forgotten and sinister institution. My call a few days ago had been taken by the departing lodger while the landlady was out, and she mistakenly thought the room had gone. I thought of how many flat-hunters she must have sent away. I wouldn't have been the only call. I wouldn't have been the first. All those people would have grabbed the room if she'd said yes or the landlady had come home and taken over, but the landlady didn't and the lodger said no, many times all afternoon. The room sat unclaimed in Fenella Boxtree's emporium of inexplicable rage. Until I arrived.

I settled in the mansion flat with my boyfriend. I worked in the Fulham deli and scoured the *Guardian* job ads for a way into creative London. I wrote applications for magazines, book publishers, any job that required care with words. Everyone was after these jobs.

I tried an employment agency. 'I want to work in the arts,' I said.

'You don't stand a chance,' said the agent, 'because you're working in a shop, so that's your CV.' She also marked me down for the other ends-meet jobs I'd done as a student. Chambermaid. Kitchen porter. In her mind, that's all I was good for. 'Have you done sweeping?' she said, ready to type that into my record.

I refused to answer.

In the shop in Fulham, my soul shrivelled every time a customer looked at me as merely a dispenser of sandwiches and change.

But then, in the local paper, among the ads for cat-sitters and church fetes, my landlady spotted this. *Proof readers wanted. No experience necessary.*

I started the following Monday. It was a tiny

publishing company that couldn't afford an ad in the national press. They weren't put off by the jobs I'd done to survive. The job was minimum wage, proofing a five-volume directory of degree courses. It was monotonous. Hundreds of pages of lists, all soporifically similar, but that didn't matter. I was making a book, an actual book that a person would take off a shelf and read and use. I thrived there, got a proper editorial job and learned all the bookish trades.

I wouldn't have found that job if I hadn't been in that flat and seen that tiny, missable advert among the local ephemera. I wouldn't have been in that flat without a string of errors and an improbable second chance. But because I was, I found people who needed the thing I could do. I found my place in London.

Unexpectedly Reavailable

The Waltons house, with its warren of empty bedrooms and mysterious hall of twelve waiting seats, is back on the market. 'Unexpectedly reavailable,' enthuses the subject line on an estate agent's email.

I think of the events that lie behind that weird phrase. People decided to have the house, named a price, clutched their hopes tightly, endured sales subterfuges that were stressful and probably unnecessary. And they won it. Its sellers began to sort and pack up, saying goodbye a hundred ways every day, looking to their next phase, reaching out with their dreams. Other dreams reached in.

Two powerful currents generating the future, the things that would happen there, the things that would no longer happen there, but would in a new place. Best times, worst times, landmark times, lazy times, life decisions, upbringings, good news, godawful news, getting through, daily grind, daily restoration, birthdays, holidays, sleeps. It is huge, this energy.

Each time one of those houses is sent to us as 'unexpectedly reavailable', the future is changing its mind. And not just about where you'll be; about who you'll be there with. Some years ago a friend was set to buy a cottage by the Thames, lost it and bought another. The two houses were just one road apart but in the catchment zones for different schools. By this bureaucratic fluke her son met classmates who are still friends, twenty years on. 'Unexpectedly reavailable' is a shaking and stirring of all the sliding doors, in the works of destiny itself.

Our future, destiny, whatever, has stalled entirely. Mick and Steph hassle Calvin because we're apparently doing nothing. We're trying our best, but we can't magic a house out of thin air. And, we have to point out, we'd be doing better if Mick and Steph hadn't lopped so much off our asking price. Calvin can choose whether to tell them that or let them do the arithmetic.

Romcom Rules: The Fallback House

Romcoms have another key character. The fallback.

We have met the fallback house.

This is a house you have a long on-off relationship with. At first you don't take it seriously, but you keep bumping into it when other good matches fall through or are betrothed elsewhere before you get a chance. That faithful fallback house will be there, still unsold.

There's nothing wrong with this house. Au contraire, it's most eligible. From the brochure we can see there are marble floors, high-end bathrooms and a handbuilt kitchen, and huge chandeliers.

One chandelier hangs in the stairwell from the top of the house to the bottom, a three-storey waterfall of dripping crystal. Another chandelier stretches along the entire length of the dining table, an overgrown crown on the ceiling. If the RMS Titanic had a teleportation room it would look like this.

The house is uncomfortably above our budget, so we can't take it seriously. But its estate agent keeps chasing us to look at it. Because it has one big handicap. Its seller hates to let people view it.

It isn't listed on Rightmove because he doesn't want strangers to see pictures of his rooms.

'He's difficult,' says the estate agent. 'He built the house himself so he's protective.' She seems to have chosen us because we have a cash offer.

This is a shy house and we have a special chance with it. Could anything be more like a romcom?

But it's too expensive, we tell the estate agent. We can't look at it.

The estate agent says: 'if it's only a question of money, you should view it'.

What should we understand by this?

We look at the house. It's impressive and well built. The finishes are very splendid and a bit unreal. The marble floors make me want to skate on them in my socks. The chandeliers are a giggle. And despite all its luxury, it's not perfect.

I say to Dave: 'There isn't a room with light from above.'

We're glad to identify this important deficiency.

Now we can forget about the house. But the estate agent keeps calling. 'Try making an offer,' she says.

Is no one else chasing this house? With every other house we're in a feverish competition.

Just for the craic, we make an offer. Just to demonstrate we are not rich enough for the Chandeliers House.

The offer is rejected.

That is surely that, but a few weeks later, the estate agent calls again. 'How are your plans?'

'We're still looking.'

The Chandeliers House is still unsold. 'Give it another try?'

What's the point? We can't pay the seller's price.

'If you offered a tiny bit more. He's keen to sell. And he still won't put it on Rightmove so you've really got a chance. He could get a much better offer if he put it online, but he won't. His personality is difficult. Come and view it again.'

We're booked to view another house nearby, so we agree. 'Those chandeliers can go,' says Dave as we walk around.

'I don't mind the chandeliers,' I say, 'but I can live without them. I can also live without those shutters and curtains because they block the light. Who puts curtains in the kitchen?'

'He's a very private person,' says the estate agent.

She keeps saying how private and difficult he is, and this is a smart angle to take with two fiction writers. We understand, very well, how peculiar

Looking

personalities can cause unexpected story outcomes. Perhaps we might, at an outside chance, get a well-made house for less than market price.

We nudge our offer up a tiny bit. It's rejected.

That's not the end.

Thus begins a long relationship.

This house will keep coming back to us.

Stuff And Nonsense

A Voyage Through Junk

It's 2006. We've lived in the house for fourteen years (twenty-two for Dave), endured its draughts and leaks, frozen in the winter, roasted in the summer, cooked dinner parties for twelve in a kitchen so cramped that the fridge has to live in the hall. We decide to grow up. Extend the kitchen. Install double glazing. Replace the boiler. Re-tile the roof and add insulation.

The roof is coming off so we have to clear the attic. There's a serious number of boxes to remove.

You might remember Dave's parents and their neighbours, who never threw things away but obviously wanted to, which is how we acquired much of our furniture. That was very handy, but years later, those neighbours are still in the habit of sending things in case we can use them. Every now and again, Dave's parents drive up from Surrey with a carload. It's all in the attic.

It can't stay. I haul out boxes of telephone answering machines, sandwich toasters, lamps, cushions, curtains and a George Foreman grill. We could outfit several productions of *Abigail's Party*. There are paintings, landscapes in faux-Constable or van Gogh.

Clutter-clearing is dangerous for daydreamers. I pause and think how, when I was a kid, every house had paintings like these, and you never noticed the picture because it was fighting with wallpaper and a horrible frame.

In one box I find several men's office shirts, still in the wrapping. Who thought we might need those? Dave has never worn suits. Out they go, for Oxfam.

I reach a big box, deep and square, the size of a washing machine. I know it's been there a long time. I've glimpsed it whenever I've ventured in to stash a kind gift of useful doodah. I've never looked in it. It's thickly covered in moth-coloured dust that matches the underside of the roof, as if the house has somehow laid it like an egg. If we weren't having to move everything, I wouldn't be touching it.

The topmost item is a fake fur. Fake fur doesn't age well. This is like the corpse of a Muppet. I whip it into a bin bag. Next is a heap of fabric in Astroturf green. I shake it out. It's a tunic with brown strips of ribbon. A leprechaun's negligee? Then a scarlet frilly cancan dress, full of pins, in the process of alteration. Then a substantial heap of fine grey net.

Is this somebody's fancy dress box? A dressmaker's work-in-progress box? Why have we got it?

The grey net has hems. And seams. I turn it around and over, trying to make sense of its structure. There's a zip. And no pins. It's a finished garment.

I find straps and it falls into place from my fingers. It has a bodice and a long, layered ballerina skirt.

It's a ballgown.

This is miraculous. I actually have need of a ballgown. For my birthday we're going to a ball at a friend's old college. I'm counting on Oxfam for the dress because the house keeps finding ways to be unexpectedly expensive.

The creases in the grey ballgown fall out, even though it has been crushed down in this box, under a dead Muppet, for decades.

What size is it? There are no labels. No labels of any kind. It must be handmade. And it's very wearable, in a dignified colour of pewter grey with tiny embroidered white sprigs, different on each layer of the ballerina skirt. How did it get here? Whose is it?

There's something else in the box. A pink and silver sheath dress. This isn't handmade. It has a label: Frank Usher.

At that moment, I know exactly who left the grey

net dress. Dave's first fiancée. She was a pattern cutter for Frank Usher. The same fiancée who left wall hangings and wineglasses as though she intended to move back in. And racy, lacy, satin lingerie in the wardrobe and airing cupboard, to disconcert any girls who dared to take her place.

It seems she has left one final surprise. A handmade ballgown.

I would not have been thrilled to find it in the early days. I would not have tried it on. And Dave might not have been thrilled to see me sweep down the stairs in it to twirl in front of the mirror. Because — and this is the second miracle — it fits me.

'Was that really hers?' he says. 'I don't remember her wearing it, but I don't know which shirt I put on this morning.'

The dress goes to the ball. Years later, it's still going to balls, weddings, parties, Christmases and New Years. The dress the house kept for me, disguised under manky remnants in a horrible box, until the day I'd be entirely happy to find it.

Try Not To Have A Piano

The world is full of unwanted pianos. You'll discover this if you try to get rid of one.

My piano has to go. As we clear the house for the builders, we can only keep things that are worth moving out and moving in again.

I used to play this piano a lot. But now the tuning is wrecked. It has gradually become a bookshelf instead. Sometimes I clear the books off, open the lid and play but I have to forgive the flatness. One day I notice it's developed a new problem. Some of the notes are now dumb. While I can accept the tuning as discordantly jazzy, I can't ignore the gap in the sound.

Still, the piano is a substantial machine. All that wood and iron and ivory and strings. It still works, largely. Surely it's of use to someone. And I'll give it away free. While the builders bash the house around, I advertise the piano. This is 2006, before Freecycle, so I try noticeboards at work and at my gym.

No takers. Not even a local school or a church.

Seriously, no one wants it? When I was a kid, pianos were everywhere. In most rooms in my school. In village halls. It seemed to be a law: a piano shall be put in any room where people gather. Here I have a piano, going free. There must be a room that needs it.

We move out of the house, leaving the piano in the hall while the builders to and fro. After a month, the piano is still there and it can't stay. 'You could,' says the project manager, 'get the council to pick the piano up with the rubbish.'

The rubbish? The piano is rubbish?

But no one wants it. I bite back my objections and check with the council. Yes, they'll take old furniture away, including pianos.

On collection day, our builders carry the piano outside and leave it in the front garden.

'We can't take the piano,' says the council, 'because the front garden has steps.'

The piano is now outside in the rain. There is no worse thing to do to a piano.

When we next visit, the lid is up. Passers-by have given it a tickle. Is this a reprieve? Maybe someone will sneak it away in the night. I hear how a DJ at BBC Radio London found a piano abandoned by the road, pushed it to the studio and it's now played on air by music's great and good. Its tone has a well-used bedspringy growl, a Tom Waits of pianos, but it's fit and working. If that piano can find a rescuer, mine surely can.

Nobody rescues my piano. I pay a clearance contractor to take it away, and they charge me £150 because of the steps.

When I was growing up, our house had a piano. The lid was kept closed and it was largely disregarded, except by me. I ambled around the keys and taught myself how scales worked, how chords worked, how to play tunes I knew. In my teen years, I discovered Kate Bush and realised I wanted to do what she did — to express the beautiful weirdness of the world.

This endeavour was too serious and private for family ears. I stopped playing unless I was alone in the house, then rushed to the instrument and let the thunder out. One day my brother sprang into the room cackling. He'd been hiding upstairs. No one can mortify you like a younger brother.

Before I became secretive and teenage, I didn't mind being listened to. I remember an evening with my father. 'Can you play the Moonlight Sonata?' he said.

I played the famous beginning. I was proud I could do that. But it was only the beginning, because I was only nine.

My father told me that when he was a child in 1930s London, his father would play the piano. Grandfather wasn't a warm family man. He had a terrifying temper and spent most of his time at work or in church, but at the piano he became a lulling presence in the house, playing late into the evening as my father and his siblings drifted to sleep.

One of his pieces was the Moonlight Sonata.

I played the beginning and my father said: 'I think the next bit goes like this'. He hummed.

'Like this?' I played.

'Yes, but up at the end. Then like this. Ba-da-da ba-da-da.'

Like kids making up a tune, he ba-dummed and I played until we had a piece that was not much like Beethoven, but something with a beginning, middle and end. We were bringing it down through memory like a family story, accurate in some details, guessed in others, Moonlight from those evenings in the 1930s, when my father and his siblings were the age I was now.

Years later when I had a flat, I decided homes needed pianos. I bought a reconditioned honkytonk that had the name Schönberg stencilled on its lid for gravitas. It was heavy as a car. The delivery crew gave me gravitas when they had to carry it up two sets of stairs and around a tight corner. They nearly left it in the kitchen.

I thought that was the only angst it would give me, but then I had it tuned. The tuner replaced a couple of pegs, warned me it would need regular and expensive maintenance. The strings were too old to hold concert pitch so he set it in its own register, in tune only with itself. I took singing lessons and my singing teacher, who had absolute pitch, refused to play it.

I played it a lot. I whiled away hours in enjoyable noise. I wrote songs with nice melodies and disappointing lyrics. I couldn't make lyrics say what I wanted.

Getting the Schönberg up the stairs to the flat had been an ordeal. So was getting it down when I went to live with Dave. He brought his five burliest friends, who lifted it over the banisters, inched it down the stairs, heaved it into the back of a van and gave me gravitas. Dave and I squashed in beside it for the journey home, playing Chopsticks around the South Circular. The jolting journey nuked its tuning for good. I thought, with guilt, of the advice from the tuner. It would need a lot of maintenance. I hadn't had him back in case he renewed more pegs at alarmingly prices. I'd get by without tuning. The instrument was just my indulgence. It didn't have to be perfect.

Regardless of its squiffy pitch, it was still a glorious force-field of sound. For the first time, as I played, words came out of the music. They weren't lyrics. They were prose, about a character who was lost unless she could play. I wasn't a songwriter after all. I was a storyteller.

My novel, my new vocation, took residence in my

brain. I hankered to play the piano too, but there was no time. The piano became a useful place to put books that had just been bought and hadn't found their way to proper shelves. Occasionally I cleared it off and played. I thought its tuning couldn't get worse, but now it was the right notes sounding in the wrong order, as Eric Morecambe would say. Then the hammers started to seize and one or two notes fell silent. This caused me much distress. I didn't know it might deteriorate like that.

When the day came to get tough on stuff, the Schönberg left us, as rubbish. I still find that hard to believe. Really, nobody needed it? Was scrapping the only option?

Fast forward. My father dies. For years he has been estranged from much of his family and there is a cohort of cousins I never had a chance to know. I met some of them when I was very small. I have never met the others. Now I'm in my fifties and they are a string of names in my deep childhood wiring, almost mythical. With the magic of the internet, I find them. They are lovely. It is profoundly strange that we all have the same eyes, jawlines and smiles. And when we mention grandfather Charlie and grandmother Winnie, we all mean the same people.

One of my cousins mentions he inherited grandfather Charlie's piano and it needs a new home.

You might already be saying: Roz, stop. Stop and think. But something has glanced across my grave. A beam of moonlight.

This is the same piano my father heard in the 1930s as he and his siblings went to sleep. They are no longer with us to give us their memories. But the piano is.

I'm a storyteller. I look for rightness and destiny. This piano, whose existence is like a miraculous plot revelation, needs a new guardian. Long ago it travelled into dreams. It belongs with people who know whose dreams they were. And it is coming to me as part of a remarkable reunion, as if it was meant to be.

It is also, says my storyteller soul, a rare symbol. Many of the stories my father told about grandfather Charlie weren't happy. There were violent outbursts. People were knocked across rooms. I remember many stories of those, and not many that were gentle. Except for the Moonlight Sonata on the piano, the lullaby of their evenings. It stands out as a memory of safety and contentment, a bridge over troubled water. Perhaps it was where Charlie, who is in my DNA as much as his offspring, also found peace.

I know about making music to find peace and sort out the world. I know how to treat a piano.

No I don't. I am a person who had a piano, who put it out in the rain as scrap. I know what I'm like. When I bought the Schönberg, I thought music would be my special vocation. It would be if I had two lives, but now I'm a writer of books.

But the story is so right. It has such perfect continuity.

What is the make of the piano? I ask.

A Blüthner, says my cousin.

Try Not To Have A Piano

Why did I ask its name? That makes things worse. No, it makes things better. I regret that I didn't take care of the Schönberg. But there's no one to reproach me but myself. Imagine if the piano I had to dump was the Blüthner.

I don't want the Blüthner to leave our family. But I'm not the person who can save it.

Also, the old piano took up a lot of space and my cousins have bigger houses. A new piece of stuff, especially one so awkward, is not sensible for Dave and me. Because we are moving.

Dragon Warriors Ride Again

Dave is the co-creator of several roleplaying games. Most were developed in this house. These walls have seen the inception, play-testing, writing, proofing and publishing pains of several series that went into the world and became treasured parts of people's childhood escapes and escapades. One of them is Dragon Warriors, released in the mid-1980s, and if you're of a certain generation and persuasion, its name will give you palpitations.

Dragon Warriors was developed by Dave with his friend Oliver. Four decades later, Dave and Oliver are still friends.

Oliver is clearing his aunt's flat so Dave helps him move the furniture.

They set off in the early afternoon. When I next hear from them, it's 10pm. True to their gaming roots, they have turned a simple trip into an epic, and one that includes all the roleplaying adventure story tropes.

Trope 1 is Hateful Vehicle. Oliver can't make the hired van reverse. Neither can Dave, but Dave doesn't know how to drive so he's excused. They park the van and load it, then can't get out of the parking space.

Dave goes to the bonnet and pushes, but the van, stuffed with furniture, is like pushing a house. So Oliver also goes to the bonnet and pushes and this is fun because — you might have noticed — no one is inside the van and steering. Trope 2, Use of Prayers.

Trope 3 is Quest for Elixir. On the route back to London, the Hateful Vehicle blares a sudden warning. *Give me AdBlue in the next fifteen miles or I won't start again.*

Oliver and Dave call the van hire firm to seek advice. What is AdBlue? Get it from a garage, they're told. (Consulting The Oracle, Who Does Not Care About Their Troubles.) They stop at a garage, obtain and administer AdBlue, use prayers again and also curses.

Next is Voyage Into the Underworld. At 9.30pm, which is much later than they planned, they reach the Big Yellow Storage facility. It is dark and spooky. The staff have long gone. There are mysterious instructions to gain entry through automated systems. (Civilisation Has Gone And Only The Robots Remain.) If they get in, will the robots let them out again? Technology hasn't so far been obliging. Also, there is torrential rain (The Elements Are Punishing You).

Treasure Becomes a Burden and Nemesis. Oliver opens the storage unit. It is already full because Oliver wants to move house and has decluttered. He must now take the vanload home, which will not please his wife. (Returning Home In Disgrace.)

But the Hateful Vehicle won't start. It's demanding AdBlue again, even though it's already got a tankful. There is a garage nearby but the rain is biblical and the walk is you-must-be-joking.

Dave phones me. As he tells me the day's adventures, I can hear Oliver talking to a call centre, which isn't going well (Consulting the Oracle, Whose Advice Makes No Sense). Dave sounds like he's having an excellently amusing time.

Dave tells me they have googled AdBlue and it's mostly composed of urea. (Character moment. Will the DM let you improvise, especially as it will entertain the other players? Roll a D6.)

An engineer arrives (The Elders Send Help). 'You shouldn't have given it AdBlue,' he says. 'It's formed crystals in the whatnot.' (Advice From Oracle Was Wrong After All.)

Oliver and Dave abandon the Hateful Vehicle, still packed with aunt's furniture, and also an urn that contains the ashes of Oliver's mother (Whiff Of Death).

The van is parked moronically across several spaces because it won't reverse. It's sagging on its axles, a blatant advertisement that it is loaded with stuff.

'It might get stolen,' says Oliver to Dave as they splosh away. 'And you know what, I don't sodding care.'

A Little Book Problem

I'm not looking forward to moving our books.

When the kitchen was extended and the roof repaired, we moved a lot of our stuff to Dave's mother's house. We started on the books early, transporting them in car loads every week.

When we moved back, we used a removal company who were famed for their cheeriness. Our books, which were moved down in months and had to come back in one day, broke their spirit. Even with Dave and me helping, it was torture. Box box box box box box, all of them heavy like parcels of housebricks.

A Little Book Problem

For the first hour we joked about how boring it was until no one could stand to hear that any more. For the rest of the hours after that, we trudged with lobotomised stares. I was reminded of pictures from my junior school history book of Egyptians building the Great Pyramid, block by block, day after day after day, for a hundred years.

Dave and I resolved we would regularly cull our books.

This hasn't gone well. Sixteen years on, every room has bookshelves and they're bursting.

I do exercise classes in the lounge on an app, staring at book spines as I grind out the reps, thinking, can any of those go? I can't part with any of the books I've enjoyed. I want to see them on the shelves. Or any of the books I didn't enjoy, because there's something to learn from them if I look at them again. Or the books I bought as research for novels I've now published. I might not read them again, but they bring back times of discovery and wonder.

They seem to breed, and some of it is our own doing. Dave has been writing a new gamebook series. He's had translation deals for other series. As if we didn't have enough trouble with our books, they're now arriving in Italian, Spanish, French and Bulgarian.

Before Us. After Us. Without Us

The Old Kingdom

In 2006, when we decide to enlarge the kitchen and fix the roof, we have to negotiate with a neighbour. He is worried our extension will block his light.

We take him our plans. He lives around the corner in a Victorian house now converted into flats.

He's a collector of vintage furniture. In his kitchen is a wooden mantelpiece just bought from eBay. We chat. He seems reassured. His other hobby is local history, and here his real beef emerges.

'Your house and the other three next to it,' he says, 'are built on the garden of this house. At one time, my garden was huge, it stretched all the way down the road. If I won the lottery I'd buy this whole building back. And your house and all the others, and I'd get rid of them.'

Really, that's the problem. Not our extension, but the very existence of our house. If you live in the place with the older boundaries, those are what you see. The old kingdom, invaded and stolen. In another country, such feelings are starting wars.

Our house sits on the other side of his fence, minding its own business. We were unaware it was the focus of such rumination and ire.

It's Not About You

A friend in America says: 'Why do you need to move? It's always good to have a home in London, and your house is so nice, so unusual.'

But it's in the wrong place.

'Shouldn't you hang on for longer?' he says. 'Neighbourhoods go up as well as down.'

It's not the neighbourhood. It's London. That's not where we live our lives now.

The longer you're in a house, the more it belongs to the people who like to visit you there.

We are also guilty of this. We have friends in Somerset whose house is a legend. You enter through an arched gate in a hedge. Inside is a valleyed garden with a row of quaint joined cottages, with a twinkly curved window and smoke curling upwards, like a children's picture book.

It feels like it fell off the edge of time. Passing cars are rare. Sirens, car alarms, house alarms, rattling trucks, roaring buses are never heard. The main road is several miles away. The sounds of the house are birds, the rustle of trees, the babbling brook and the neighbour's chickens.

Inside there are tantalising glimpses of its history, for it is nearly 400 years old. There's a bread oven dug into one wall, from when the house was the village bakery. The bathroom is a wonder. A claw-footed roll-top tub as long as a car. Giant-mouthed taps like the controls for a waterfall. Wallpaper of delicate Chinese figures in brown and green. It's period wallpaper, but what period? Older than anyone knows.

Our friends moved here in the 2000s. They came on holiday from inner-city Brighton and decided to stay. After a despairing search in which nothing they could afford was suitable they happened on this, a probate house, unmodernised since the previous owners bought it fifty years before. It needed intensive care for damp. An outside wall had to be pulled straight and stabilised with steel. Its low doorways were a constant danger as the family are uniformly tall, so the ground floor had to be dug down. But this house of great, organic age, in its own valley, fits them so well. They are artists and gardeners, and have filled it with their paintings, statues, ceramics, flower arrangements, sculptures and musical instruments. Some of these are hewn from logs and branches in the surrounding woods. The house completes them, and they complete it.

When we arrive to visit, it is just as we remember it, and more enchanting as the years pass. It still requires a sense of adventure. The downstairs loo is in a shed in the garden. For many years the shed had no roof. We would nip out, shivering and yelping, return to the warm, giggling.

When we leave, it's with invitations to come back soon, and we will. Meanwhile, we know it's there, and they are there too, at the helm.

They may not stay for ever. The children are now grown up and have moved away. The house is cranky, and throws surprises that require a brave look at the bank account. And if they decide to sell the dismay will be felt far and wide.

The Homecoming Surprise

There's a trope in stories that the hero returns home to find an unexpected change. His sister is getting married. His cat has adopted the neighbours. It's the skip in the record that confirms time has passed, the story has continued without him.

When Dave and I return after time away, we look for the change. There's always a thing, though we hope it's not drastic. The tree cut down, so the house behind it looks naked. The shop that's repainted or closing. The new roadworks, which will change the traffic soundscape while we're indoors, doing daily things.

Then we settle. We've confirmed this place continued to have adventures while we were elsewhere, acquired a few more wrinkles as we also have, and now we turn the key and align again, back in step.

Intruders

It's October 1998. 6pm. Arriving home from work, I turn the key in the mortice lock, then in the top Yale. Something holds the door, low down. The bottom bolt is on.

That is strange. We never use that bolt except last thing at night. And Dave is out.

Someone is in the house and has bolted the door from inside.

I hear noises. Bumps. I know the house's sounds, and this is someone on the stairs.

More noises. Now this is someone running on the stripped floorboards of the ground floor.

That's odd and wrong.

I ring the bell. The sounds intensify. A panicked escalation like an animal disturbed in a hedgerow. I put my eye to the letterbox and flip it open. A bag is in the hall.

The bag is a big holdall, which I recognise as ours. It contains one of the speakers from the hi-fi.

We are, right now, being burgled.

I lean on the doorbell, hard. You've been caught, you bastards. I'm here. You'd better scuffle and scrabble right out the way you came in. That's my speaker you're trying to take, which I bought when I was a student.

I lean on the bell. I don't know what else to do. It's before the days of mobiles so I can't call the police. I don't want to run to a phonebox. I want to stay here, defending my house, tormenting the people inside. Ring. Ring. You've been caught. I'm here. You're in my house and now you get out.

A friend arrives. Not a neighbour. We don't know our neighbours (remember this is London). But tonight friends are arriving because Dave is having his fortnightly roleplaying game. Now Ian is here, thank God.

I speak in a rasping whisper. 'There's someone in the house. Though it's gone quiet now.'

Ian peers into the front windows. I haven't thought of doing that. I haven't dared.

Ian quietly drops his satchel of roleplaying books and character sheets, goes to the side gate, which is as tall as he is, and nimbly climbs over.

Blimey, I didn't know it was possible to climb that gate. Be careful.

I wait. It is quiet in the house now. No, I can hear a bit of running. God, Ian, don't get hurt. I hear more sounds. Footsteps on the bare-boards floor. Confident footsteps, which know they're permitted to be there, coming to the front door. The bolt at the bottom of the door is slid back and the door is opened. Ian is there, carrying a replica samurai sword we keep in the hall. Roleplaying games have trained him well.

'They broke a side window to get in, but they've gone now. And it's all right. They haven't made a mess.'

God bless Ian.

Dave arrives. We search around. Except for the window, there is no damage. No drawers upended out of spite. We can trace the burglars' passage through the house. They went straight to the top bedroom. Searched the wardrobe. A couple of holdalls are on the floor by the bed. They're empty. The burglars must have been selecting them for the getaway. Several bags, which must mean several burglars. We are following their plan. Their plan of ransack.

Dave's printer has gone. The printer has always been trouble. We are amused at the trouble it will give its recipients. Look what you got, bastards. Don't steal our stuff.

Back on the ground floor in the hall is the bag they left, which I saw from the letterbox. The bag that contains one of the hi-fi speakers. The other speaker has gone and one is no good without the other. The speakers hadn't given us trouble. We enjoyed their rich, wall-trembling sound. That theft is an outrage. Those speakers are the first grown-up thing I bought when I was at college, with money I should have used for books or breakfasts.

And the burglars probably broke the other speaker as they escaped. The only route out, if they can't come out of the front, is over the back wall, into another garden. That garden is five feet lower than ours, a nice long fall they wouldn't be expecting. Maybe they broke themselves as well as their loot. I hope they did.

Don't invade our house. Our fury will have no limits.

The rest of the gamers arrive. They find us giving statements to the police. And thanking a guy who has boarded up the window. Licking the house's wounds.

Wine is opened. The game gets under way. I usually go upstairs and write while the game is in progress. Games aren't my thing. But I can't write tonight. I stay with the noise and the people. Friendly noise. Invited noise. Normal Thursday things to banish the intruder spirits who bashed their way in, went through our rooms, decided what they wanted and took it.

I keep rerunning the outrage. I settle and then I remember. What if they took the bracelet Dave gave me as an engagement present? What if they took my CD Walkman? I run upstairs to check things as I think of them. All are still there, undisturbed. Back down to the game, which is becoming quite a party. We fill the house again with the noise of friendships and people who've been coming here for years and are always welcome.

Numerology

'Don't bother with a landline when you move,' says a friend.

Then he adds: 'But I still remember your number off by heart so it'd be a shame to lose it. I used to know loads of phone numbers. I only know four these days. My mobile, my wife's mobile, my dad's landline and yours.'

Reading The Room

I am bookish, not numberish. At school, I was bored and baffled by maths. But I never minded the maths lessons because they took place in a room with a beautiful ceiling. Ornate cornices with curling leaves; a ring of plaster flowers that had once surrounded a chandelier.

The school buildings were a group of three grand houses that had originally been the homes of wealthy Victorian businessmen, with servants' staircases, butlers' pantries, morning rooms, drawing rooms and stable blocks. They still carried relics of their finery. Doors panelled with Venetian glass or flanked by granite columns. Fireplaces, their carvings blurred under annual coats of white gloss paint. When maths defeated me, I looked around and read the room. In this place a family once received guests, or learned awful secrets over dinner, or made life-changing pacts at midnight over port.

One of these buildings was a pair of funereal Addams Family semis with high gaunt gables. The buildings were joined by doors through the connecting wall so you could cross to the mirror side. Pop through and it was reverseworld with the staircase on the right instead of the left, where you might catch your reflection running upwards. When I was very small, my violin lessons were on the top floor of this building. I spent a lot of time getting lost on the wrong side, not always accidentally.

Each house had sprawling grounds, and our school day involved crossing from garden to garden by a series of whimsical portals. A hole in a hedge took you from the junior classrooms and choir practice rooms into the corner of next door's lawn, along an ornamental shrubbery to the second old house which had some of the subject rooms, the dining hall and the sixth form, then a 1970s block of labs and classrooms with bare brick walls and green lino tiles like a police station. After this brief blot came a long set of steps down a steep Victorian rockery, because the gloomy Addams Family houses (the gym, art studio, more classrooms and tiny garrets for violin teachers) sat at the bottom of a plunging valley. In the 1970s a bridge was built from the ground floor of the police block across the chasm to come in on the first floor of Addams Family.

In the last year of junior school, we had our lessons in a spartan warren of attics at the top of one of the houses. These were once the servants' bedrooms, a sanctuary after a long day for people who probably didn't have many private moments. Here we were, a herd of girls plonking our bags on the desks, scraping chairs along the floor, making our hubbub. Hundreds of us over the years, clamouring through the space. But once upon a time these rooms were quieter, used by a small number of people who were all part of one family kingdom, all joined in one story.

In 2020s London now, around the corner from our house, is a school. It has bought a small block of 1960s flats to convert into classrooms. I pass it often. The school is using the minibus to clear away the apparel of personal spaces: plasterboard walls, fireplaces, light fittings, kitchen cabinets, bathroom sinks, radiators, wardrobes. Some of the school pupils will have seen this too. They will have walked past the building in earlier times when every window showed different curtains and posters and stuff, or they will have seen it from their school grounds over the fence. It has always been another country, a country of unseen stories of real lives. One day it will open to them.

I wish them many happy daydreams.

A Pilgrimage

Near our house, a Victorian psychiatric hospital is being redeveloped as smart apartments. It's in the grounds of an NHS complex that I drive past every day. I thought it was only modern blocks, but one afternoon there was a builder's screen with intriguing pictures of what lay further in — an age-blackened Tudor-style building like Hampton Court, rows of characterful windows bronzed by the sunrise.

The traffic on that road is slow. Plenty of time to study the pictures. The banners showed apartments where radiant, modern people basked in sunlit rooms.

But this building couldn't always have been so happy. Who originally stood at those windows? What sea of troubles brought them here, to retreat from complication, come to terms with themselves?

And then I made an astonishing discovery. One of those people was my own grandmother, my father's mother.

She was Winnie, wife of Charlie who played the Moonlight Sonata on the Blüthner piano. Winnie died several years before I was born, and also before most of my cousins were born. She is a mysterious figure to us. We know her mainly by fragments of her story, and her story is tragic.

When Winnie was four years old, she witnessed her mother trying to cut her father's throat with a carving knife. Winnie's mother then turned the knife on herself. After that, Winnie's father disappeared, her mother went to Broadmoor high-security psychiatric hospital and Winnie was brought up by relatives, who, according to the accounts we have, may not have been kind.

Some details we're not sure of. Winnie might have witnessed her baby sister die of an illness. Her father may have been run out of town by his in-laws, or let his family think he'd died.

Perhaps I was told more about her when I was a child. If so, I remember little of it. Adults were always talking to me about people I could not put a face or a physical presence to. They seemed to swim in a past full of unattached names; old friends, old colleagues, relatives. Whether these people were alive or dead, related to me or not, I couldn't keep up. Children are good at pretending they've understood. I was too young to know I'd want to understand about Winnie one day.

I do remember the story about the throat-cutting. It was so bizarre and frightening. I also saw a sadness when my father talked about Winnie, a fragility that warned the past could be a dark place, and the mind could easily break itself.

I was easily spooked as a child. I wanted to avoid darkness. I didn't ask more.

Now I've reconnected with my cousins and we've talked about Winnie. They know little more than I do, so perhaps there wasn't much talk about her after all. That generation didn't share, especially about mental fragility. But one impression is clear: a sense that people didn't know what to do for her, and carried this regret even after she died.

My cousins and I are building a Dropbox folder of family pictures and documents. One day, I scan some death certificates left by my father. Winnie's is there, and that's when I notice. Her place of death is Springfield Hospital, south London.

That old psychiatric hospital just down the road from our house, now being stripped for stylish modern living.

It is astounding that Winnie was here, because her home with Charlie was far away, on the opposite side of London. To make that journey takes several hours. How did she end up almost on my doorstep? Close the distance of decades, overlay 1961 on 2021, and there she is, standing at those tall windows as I pass on Burntwood Lane outside, almost every day. As I sit in my house, there are people of her DNA and mine, including my father, making the pilgrimage to visit her. It was a frequent pilgrimage; she was there many months. They would arrive at the station I use, pass the routine landmarks that tell me I'm nearly home, pass the end of my road, pass my house, which is near the corner. Pass me, in another part of time.

Why did my father not mention it? He always set great store by coincidence and destiny. His belief in this was like a religion. If he was upset or worried, he would search for a coincidence as reassurance and comfort. Often he had to be very determined to find these coincidences. When he fell out with a longtime friend, he told me it wasn't the end because the digits in their two phone numbers added up to the same total, which meant harmony would be restored. It was the only coincidence he could unearth and he must have worked a long time to find it, like someone determined to make a stubborn machine work. He made much of it, as if it was a sign from the universe, yet he never mentioned the clear and non-contrived coincidence of where I lived and where his mother died. But now I remember that when he visited me in London, he came to our house just once, then preferred to meet in the centre of town. Maybe because he liked a chance to visit central London. Maybe because he preferred, as I did, to avoid darkness.

Now, in 2021, Springfield is about to erase the past.

One Saturday, when the construction workers aren't there, I go in.

I pass the NHS hospital. The Victorian wards stand behind, dark with age and neglect, watched over by cranes. I stand for a long while beside a garden wall that looks like it has come from a more forbidding time. It is as thick as a gun emplacement, sundered by jagged cracks. There are rows of greenhouses that look old. I have read that patients were encouraged to garden. Perhaps Winnie did this when she was here.

I approach the building. Lights are on in the upper storeys. I peer through a window whose frame is freckled with rust. I see a dark space and my own reflection.

Beside a drainpipe, I find a heap of pillows. It is startling, strange and unexpectedly intimate.

I am considering the pillows when a voice calls out. A security guard.

Maybe if I tug his heartstrings he'll show me around. 'My grandmother died here in the 1960s,' I tell him. Such a phrase should, I think, be an absolute passport to anywhere I like. It worked for a similar situation in *Not Quite Lost*.

The guard gives me a suspicious look. 'This is private property.'

'Sorry! Is there someone I can talk to?'

He notices my camera. 'You can't take pictures here.'

I slip my camera into my pocket. He'd better not try to make me delete my pictures. In case he does, I say: 'I have a family connection here that I never knew about,' and try to look overwhelmed.

'You can't take pictures here,' he says again, 'because of the CCTV.'

Because of the CCTV? I understand he has to do his job, but I don't understand that reasoning.

The guard walks me to the gate. Sorry I can't be more adventurous, but I'm a writer, not a ninja urban explorer. And I don't want him to start thinking about my unauthorised pictures.

At home, I find the developer's website with a video of the interior. An arched, panelled entrance hall, painted a chilly blue. Long corridors and a chapel, littered with fallen plaster. An empty ward full of slanted light, with those windows. The floor is marked with chalk for conversion into an apartment, the outlines of new rooms. Dining area. Lounge.

My own pictures are less dramatic, but I'm glad I have gone there, stood in the grounds, before its old purpose is tidied away.

All those names we hear when we're children. They are remote facts, hard to grasp as people, let alone people who are threaded into our blood. We need to be older to develop real curiosity about them and by then there might be no one left to ask. I know Winnie only by a few memorable and frightening events and the note of helplessness in my father's voice. As a person she will always be an enigma. What was she good at, what did she laugh at, what did her voice sound like?

I pass the hospital on my routine comings and

goings. The pictures of the historic façade are unchanged, though the old wards, the chapel, the day rooms, will be disappearing. The spaces where a lost soul looked out of a window and considered her life. Although I am decades late, this is my pilgrimage. I never knew Winnie, but this place did.

Weirdstoned: Under Alderley Edge

When I was a small child in my quiet northern village, I learned that the woods near our house had a hidden underworld.

It started when we had visitors and my parents took us all for a walk. We came to a gap in the trees and an area sealed off with barbed wire. Behind the wire was a clearing of bald rock with a long gash into darkness, as if a catastrophe had split the ground open.

'That's one of the old copper mines,' said my mother. There was a hint of warning in her voice, and everyone else said 'ah', as though they agreed. We moved on.

I walked with my head turned nearly backwards, focused on that raw ragged hole in the earth.

After that, I pestered my parents for information about the mines. Where else were they? Nowhere near here, I was told. Did our garden have secret tunnels? It did not, perish the thought. The mines, I was informed, were a long way from the house so I didn't need to worry about them.

Worried? That was not my feeling at all. And I soon discovered the mines weren't far away. The farmer in the next field had a mine entrance on his land. Sometimes I'd see people in overalls and helmets gathered around a manhole in the corner of his horse paddock. I thought about the thrilling chaos of the mine in the woods. Under this innocent pasture were chambers of unknown shapes and unknowable size. If only I could x-ray the ground.

The mines in Alderley Edge date back at least as far as the early Bronze age. This was staggering to me. While we lived our 1970s lives on the surface in the light, occupied with school and other average stuff, this labyrinth lay below, an ancient geography started aeons ago by people following seams laid down in the founding movements of the earth itself. If you can't feel the mystery in that, check you have a pulse. The mines closed in the 1920s, but they were still there, an otherland under our feet, dark, empty and waiting.

Then at school, we read *The Weirdstone of Brisingamen* by Alan Garner, a fantasy story of two children who are drawn into an Arthurian quest with sleeping knights, ancient beings and wizards, and a terrifying underworld. That underworld was our mines. Alan Garner knew them personally; he grew up in Alderley Edge and so did his ancestors. His Weirdstone novel put the mines into a tale of legend and magic. It seemed to understand my thirst to know these dormant places, full of old time.

In one chapter called Plank Shaft, the children cross a chasm on a narrow beam of wood while the evil svart-alfar, the deep dwellers, blink far down in the gloom. The Plank Shaft, I discovered, was real. One day, a photographer from the local newspaper went down one of the mines and took pictures. There was also a Sphinx Chamber and a Chain Shaft.

I kept the article about the shafts and the chamber. I looked at it often.

I grew older. I was trusted to roam without climbing into stupid places. Alderley Edge is named because it's on a high ridge of land, the Edge. If you crossed the road from our house and walked to the end of a path, suddenly the trees dropped away and there was sky, and an aircraft-eye view across several counties of fields and forests and farms. Paths led downwards. Stone wells had been built beside the paths, collecting run-off from the slopes. A rock bulged above one of the wells, carved with verses and a picture of a sinister bearded face that looked to me like the Turin shroud, which had recently been in the news. This face was the wizard, from the local legend that became Garner's novel.

With my brother and the kids who lived next door, I became a native of the woods. We learned the names of places. Castle Rock was the ridge near our house. Walk through the woods, staying on the highest ground, and you came to another ridge at Stormy Point, which had the Devil's Grave, a cave with a round hole in the roof blocked by a square block of stone, which you must not run around three times. Everyone did it, three shrieking laps.

One summer we discovered more names, when the tea shop in the old gamekeeper's cottage made maps which it sold for 10p. We learned what to call the strange pit with the straight cliff wall at one end and rhododendrons growing at the bottom. We found a druid circle and a valley with three small tunnel mouths in the rooty earth walls.

The tunnels were drainage channels from the old mines.

By now, you couldn't get into the mines by yourself. They were sealed with concrete. But this wooded valley had been missed by the safety police. We crawled into a tunnel. It was so totally dark we scuttled out at top speed, very like the Scooby-Doo gang. We even had a dog with us. As we stood shaking and laughing, the dog ran back in. Her black coat vanished in the darkness. She turned around, her eyes became two demonic copper pennies and we screamed all over again.

I found a book about the mines. They also had names. West Mine. Wood Mine. Pillar Mine. Engine

Vein Mine. Uncompromising, functional names. Engine Vein was my favourite. It could be a rock band.

Engine Vein was also the mine that started it for me, the mine behind the barbed wire on that walk long ago. A piece of danger, left in the open. The chasm into great depth that beckoned you to fall, a fall that you could never climb out of because of the hollows and overhangs. I often stopped and looked at it. It seemed milder than my memory. There wasn't even any barbed wire.

So one day I climbed in.

It wasn't a chasm. It was a trench, and you could walk along it. And it wasn't especially deep. Just a few feet higher than my head, a bit like the entrance to a grotto in a National Trust garden. It stopped in a bulge of rock. I could have sworn it went endlessly into blackness.

Had I grown so tall and wise that this thing had lost its thrill? When I showed friends around the woods, I'd say 'I used to think this was so big. Now it hardly looks frightening at all.'

The Derbyshire Caving Club announced an open day for one of the mines. My brother and I went along and joined a queue of inquisitive locals at a manhole in the woods. We were given helmets with head torches and followed the guide down. Although I knew from my reading that this mine was the least exciting, just a simple set of tunnels with no spectacular chambers or shafts, I was here at last, in the hidden parts under the forest floor, scraping my helmet on the roof, putting my hands on the mud-glistening rock. I was a firehose of questions. My guide spotted a genuine enthusiast. Come back on Wednesday evening, he said. We'll take you down a proper mine.

The mine was Engine Vein.

We arrived in darkness. A guy called Kevin gave us helmets and led us into the forest, past the gash in the ground, which was now so tame. A short distance away was a manhole cover. I'd seen the manhole cover countless times and thought it was a drain.

It wasn't a drain. It was the new entrance to the mine. We climbed down. Head torches on. First it was a brick shaft, then it became older, an organic wall of hewn rock. It opened into a big space. And there was the frightening maw from my memory and we were standing at the bottom. The staggering, awful space was still here, deep and random, formed without a care for whether you could climb out.

I hadn't imagined it. The mine really was that deep. Somewhere in the intervening years a false concrete floor had been added to make it safe.

I looked up, a long way. Far above, about the height of a cathedral, the beam of my torch found wood grain — the print of the shuttering that had supported the concrete when the floor was poured. The pattern, like panelling from a Swedish sauna, looked weirdly domestic in this untamed space.

'I usually work here on my own,' said Kevin.

The mines needed work? They did. They filled with mud over the years. Kevin showed us a tunnel he had excavated. 'That used to be completely silted up. I dug it out. It took months.'

The tunnel looked tiny, barely the height of my knees. Barely tall enough for a dog. Kevin wasn't a small bloke. He had crawled into there? I was reminded of a sequence in Weirdstone when one of the kids, Susan, has to crawl through a cramped tunnel, completely in the dark, so narrow she gets stuck. She imagines herself being trapped there until she dies, and then trapped there for the rest of time.

Kevin had crawled into a tunnel like that and slowly dug the mud out, down here on his own.

I've never been claustrophobic but I was acutely aware of the press of rock around us, how soft and bruisable we were. How dependent on headtorches and batteries. If you smashed your headtorch on the unpredictable roof or the battery died, it was you and the darkness and this solid place, which, unlike a room, didn't make spatial sense. It wasn't built in a knowable way with corners or levels or up or down. In a building, if the lights go out, you can probably find your way around. This space had no rules. If you tried to feel your way out, you'd go round the crannies, wherever they chose to take you, for ever.

Kevin worked down here alone. I couldn't spend a single second here without company.

Kevin led us down a tunnel, thankfully one we could walk in upright. The walls were glossed with russet-coloured mud. There were sounds. Dripping. The occasional skitter of falling stones. And a profound absence of other sounds. No rustling trees or night birds or passing cars in the belly of the mine. Just our footsteps and voices and the water and the shifting grit, and big silence.

'Listen,' said Kevin. 'Do you hear that? The Blue Shaft is booming.'

I couldn't hear anything I'd describe as a boom, but there was a soft echo.

'I'll take you there.'

He took us along a tunnel, stooping as the roof became lower. It ended in a hole with a thin metal ladder. As we climbed down, our torches illuminated the wall behind the rungs. The blueness was suddenly there, a blaze of brilliant sapphires and azures and cyans and cobalts and peacocks and aquamarines, all the blues you ever heard names for, brought by the mine's secret rivers and laid on the rock.

We reached the bottom and stood looking up. 'There are not many people who've climbed down the Blue Shaft,' said Kevin. He sounded proud. Probably not of our climb; the ladder made it easy. But proud of this place, only known to people who wanted to come far down into the ground.

Then Kevin knelt on the floor, put his head into a tiny tunnel and snake-squirmed in. 'This is the way out.' Oh joy, just like Susan in Weirdstone.

We followed. Again, I felt the press of rock all around, the sense of my softness in this space that is not meant to be suitable for human life, the fact I couldn't sit up or turn around.

There was a thing I used to do when I was small. If I couldn't get to sleep or was bored of being in bed, I'd turn upside down, diving under the covers and rotating my body so my feet were on the pillow and my face was where my feet should be. The covers were sheets and blankets, not a duvet, so the lower part of the bed was sealed like a parcel. It pressed tightly on my face. At the upside-down point, pinned in by the covers, I'd think, what if I never found the way out? The answer was to believe the open air still existed. Crawl and believe, and you'll find it again.

This tunnel, touching my helmet and shoulders and knees and the flats of my forearms and my chest and tummy and the tips of my digging toes, was like that.

As we crawled, I thought how men used to work like this. Not the intrepid caving volunteers who had chosen to come from curiosity. Men who had to work here, maybe without as much light as we had, maybe digging their route for the first time, maybe not knowing where they were going, aware that they might go downwards for ever. I thought how I knew nothing about courage.

We came out of the tiny tunnel, without mishaps, and returned to the main cavern. I looked up again and saw myself being hurried away from this magnetic chasm that might swallow a wandering child, an adult, a car, a double-decker bus. There are some spaces on earth that put us in our place, remind us what we need. We need light. The sounds of the world that tell us where we are and that the seconds and minutes and hours are still passing, everywhere, reliably onwards, for everyone. A knowledge of which way is up and where outside is.

Kevin took us up to the surface, then went back into the mine to work. On his own. He wasn't scared. And what was there to be scared of? The rocks moving? They didn't move. We had to do the moving, squeezing through gaps, clambering over awkward formations, finding out if they could take us. We were irrelevant and inconsequential in that world, the way an insect or a mouse must feel if it attempts to scale a piece of our furniture. And here's another addition to my list of essentials: we need other humans, humans who know where they are and what they're doing so that we can learn their confidence. And because life is a reassuring force in itself.

At the end of Weirdstone, Susan and her brother Colin emerge from the caves. Garner guides our senses back to the normal world by remarking, in a parentish way, that they are both completely plastered in the sandstone mud that washes through the caves. My brother and I were too. We were country kids, used to mud, dirt, sand, pond slime, cowpats and horse manure, but this was mud of a different order. Not the brown topsoil of the fields or the peaty leaf litter of the woods. This was sticky, mineraly and orange. The substance of the deep secret spaces under the Edge.

Weirdstoned: Thin Places

In 2018, Alan Garner releases a memoir of his childhood, *Where Shall We Run To*. When I read it I'm back on the Edge, in the places I found on my wanderings. I thought I had uniquely discovered them. But they are Alan Garner's too, and almost identically.

Here is Alan at the Devil's Grave, wondering if he dares run around it widdershins. Here he is at one of the wells, where he is taught to find a leaf, place it on the rock shiny side up, and take a drink. In the 1970s I'm taught this exact leaf trick by the next-door neighbours, who have learned it from their gardener. Their gardener's family has lived on the Edge for generations, in the gamekeeper's cottage, a gingerbread house with green window sills that is mentioned in Garner's memoir. In the 1970s it's also the tea room where we bought our maps and learned the names of the Edge.

This is like the Six Degrees of Kevin Bacon game, where the aim is to link yourself or a celebrity to the actor Kevin Bacon in six steps or fewer. If I play Six Degrees of Alan Garner, I'm there in just one step, in things he heard and said and did. I am there in his actual footsteps.

He describes a rock on the Edge with a horizontal gash like a mouth. It was terrible and also irresistible. My brother and I would discuss whether we dared to lie in there, how far we could slide in before we would be stuck for ever, whether it would close on us. Young Alan in the 1940s wriggles into the crack, commanded by its shape, and lies there, gazing into the rock which sparkles with minerals.

I am reading someone playing a game of being me, before I was born.

Here I am in the 1970s on Castle Rock, the ridge with the view across Cheshire and Lancashire. On a sunny day I can see all the way to the airport in Manchester, which is called Ringway, a name it will soon abandon. I look for the glint of sunlight on the aircraft as they take off and land. Garner, in the 1940s, is standing where I am, watching aircraft land at the

RAF Ringway aerodrome, which is not yet called just Ringway, but soon will be.

In 1945 at the end of the war, the villagers gather on Castle Rock to watch the street lights being switched back on, all the way to Manchester. Time lives in layers on this spot. Overlap me, a girl in the 1970s who is lucky to live in peacetime, and Garner, a boy in 1945 who is watching peace return. It's an experience that could come from one of his own novels, where thin places leak the visions and sounds of another time.

Go back to the 1914-1918 war and another layer is waiting. Garner tells of his father sitting on Castle Rock, seeing a Zeppelin fly over, so low and huge that everything under its belly goes dark. A hundred years later in London in 2018, I read something in his book that makes me wish I could slip back there for a closer look. In the 1970s, the rock was chiselled with names and initials. The local churchyard was like that too, paved with old gravestones, names under your feet. I used to try to read the names engraved in Castle Rock, but they were too overlapped and weathered. Now I would like one more look because one of those names was Joseph Garner. He was Alan's grandfather.

Ghosts leak from Garnertime to mine, in sounds as well as actions. Alan, at school in the 1940s, hears the village air-raid siren. Roz, in the 1970s in a French lesson, though not in the same school, is startled by a loud slow-rising wail. 'That's the air-raid siren,' says the teacher, using all her spoilsport instincts to keep the surprise out of her voice and continue the lesson, as if this noise is a completely normal thing, which it isn't. We've all been at this school for years and we've never heard it. She resumes her discussion, which is about irregular verbs, but the siren is still sounding, now descending from a wail to a growl as it settles back to sleep, and we are staring out of the window to find where it is coming from. 'Look,' says someone. 'It's on top of the Trafford Arms Hotel.' Irregular verbs have to wait until everyone has successfully seen the object, a fat red cylinder like a beer barrel in a cage on the roofline of the hotel. We never knew it was there. We don't know why it went off. 'Irregular verbs,' says the teacher, forcefully.

I have not thought about this until I'm reading Garner's book and he describes that same siren, on top of the Trafford Arms hotel, sounding over the village, and all his class standing up from their desks and filing to the shelter. A sound once full of meaning, now harmless, travelling across time, like a ghost who screams though the reason for the scream has long gone.

We all knew the house where Garner had lived, though we didn't know it was connected with him. It was a wizened little cottage with tiny windows, like a piece of something ancient left over while other houses arrived around it. It had been a tollgate, said Garner. He was growing up within those walls, for some of the time ill and confined to bed, escaping into reading and legends, mapping a world he could feel was alive around him even if he couldn't reach it. The tollgate. The gateway. Garner himself becomes the gateway.

In the 1970s, my brother is at the primary school where Garner was a pupil. Hop back in time, back past Alan Garner, and Garner's father is on that spot, building the classroom that my brother, in the 1970s, eventually sat in.

Next door to the school is the church. In the 1940s, Alan's father is gilding a cockerel weathervane for the steeple. It's so big that young Alan can sit on its back. In the 1970s, the cockerel has been in position for decades. It might remember it once had a rider, a boy who tried to see everything. It turns in the wind, high above the village, as I walk in a procession of blue-uniformed girls to the church for a choir rehearsal or an end-of-term service.

The cockerel might see us on another of our school routines, as we walk to the village sports club to play hockey. Garner's memoir also knows this club, where the 'people from the big houses went to play cricket and tennis'. Two of those big houses will become my school, though in his time they are still private homes. And this means that in the 1970s, the people coming from the big houses are us.

The cockerel might also see me as I push my bicycle up the back road to the Edge. On the steepest section, I have to stop to get my breath. One side has been cut out of the rock. There are pick-marks in the walls, feathery like diagonal hyphens, as if someone has drawn rainfall into the rock. I wonder about them as

I lean on the handlebars, breathing deep. Now I learn they were made by one of the Garners; Alan's grandfather's grandfather, who helped cut the actual road out of the hillside. He also made the Edge's wells and carved the most startling piece of Wizardry, the deep-etched face of the bearded man above the Wizard's Well, the one that looks to me like the face on the Turin shroud. In Alan's time in the 1940s all the wells had faces but by the 1970s, only this one survives.

Weirdstone showed me how, by telling stories, we can fill a place with magic. That magic might be legends and powers and elves and the numinous, as if the land has things it wants us to know. Or it might be a personal magic, the release of something already within us. When I read Garner's memoir, I see I also inherited another thing — the actual land and spaces I came from.

He lay in that split rock. So did I. He learned the same lore I learned, the leaf for drinking from, the rules of the Devil's Grave. He stood on Castle Rock as I did and looked for the planes. Distant splinters of light, in that same corner of the sky, in the 1940s and the 1970s, following the same beacons through the air.

Garner and his ancestors left beacons to follow about how to live in this place. He heard the siren across the village. So did I. Its purpose was long gone, but it was still there in readiness.

Weirdstone begins in readiness. It starts with the Alderley Edge legend, about a wizard who guards a cave of sleeping knights until they are needed again. In the real world the Edge's guardians are the Garners themselves. They have been in the village, tending the stories of its soil and stones, since 1592.

In 2020, I find a documentary made by Granada TV about Garner, *The Edge of the Ceiling*. It was broadcast in 1980, and my home is less than a mile from him as he walks a route of Castle Rock, Stormy Point, the Devil's Grave, the Wizard's Well. While he is talking, a girl rides into the background on a grey pony.

This must have been an unexpected delight for the film crew. In the Alderley Edge legend, the wizard meets a farmer with a grey horse and buys it for one of his knights. As Alan Garner explains the story, which he learned from his grandfather, here is a girl riding a grey horse, right where they are filming. They linger on her.

So do I. This is not just any girl riding a horse. I knew her.

She was one of the neighbours I explored the woods with. I sometimes groomed for her at shows. I am certain it is her; I recognise the way she fits that horse. He used to make her look petite, then that summer she became tall and leggy, as she is here. It is unmistakably them.

Until this moment, Alan's Edge and my own have been separated by decades. His memoir was remarkably and magically mine, but at a remove. I was chasing his timeline and the timelines of his forbears. Now, here is one of the people from my Edge, who also happens to be an echo from the legend behind the Edge's wells and the Weirdstone, and time collapses to put us all, at last, in the same story.

Weirdstoned: Your Old Home Is On Reality TV

Alderley Edge in the 1970s was famous to nobody, except for fans of Alan Garner. It was a Normal-NcNormal village with grocers, newsagents, a post office, schools, a supermarket, a gift shop and a quiet Chinese restaurant.

The present is another country. Now, everybody knows Alderley from bling-belt reality TV series like *Living On The Edge*, whose logline is 'LA lifestyle, Cheshire postcode'. Champagne bars (four of them), Botox clinics (three of them), high-flying footballers and low-slung Lamborghinis.

One reality show, *Sally Lindsay's Posh*

Sleepover, made an entire episode in my childhood home.

Strictly speaking, it wasn't my childhood home. It was a house built on its rubble.

I wrote about my childhood home, Edge Croft, in *Not Quite Lost*. Edge Croft was an Edwardian house high on a hill, full of period mystery, with hidden fireplaces, the shadows of formal flowerbeds in the lawns, bell-pushes that had once summoned servants and, because it was built in 1909, a stable block. My family sold Edge Croft in the 1990s, another family lived there until 2017, then the next owners brought their bulldozers.

I never thought I'd get a chance to see Edge Croft's successor except by snooping on Google. Now here it was, with its own forty-five-minute documentary.

I watched the presenter's dashcam as she drove the last mile to the house. I had not been back to the area since 1991. My old road was now hard to recognise, an avenue of expensive security gates, but the underlying waypoints were still the same. Pass an unmade road on the left. Look for the telegraph pole on the right. Find the drive immediately after.

Here was the name on the gate: Edgecroft. One word. In our day, it was two, Edge Croft. I'm a words person. That distinction is important.

Of course I was eager to dislike the new house, so you might take my remarks with a pinch of sodium chloride. But please believe me when I say Second Edgecroft didn't look in any way like a house.

It was a massive, antiseptic crate of brick and glass with a revolving door, like the headquarters of a tech corporation. In the hallway was a multi-storey glass lobby with a lift and a giant bronze rhinoceros. The new Edgecrofters, Irene and Ian, were fond of enormous metal animal sculptures. It was *The Land That Time Forgot*, in a shopping centre.

To give you an idea of its bulk and luxury level, Second Edgecroft was valued at £12 million, though First Edge Croft certainly wasn't. Don't even ask for that in arms and legs.

But I hadn't come just to sneer. I couldn't because my parents' alterations to Edge Croft, in the late 1960s, were criminal. They ripped out the twinkly paned bay windows and installed a row of bleak patio doors like a bus garage.

But a home is more than a building. Whatever brass monster zoo was now on the site, we were on the same ground, under the same sky. We were in the landscape I saw every day, from my earliest conscious years to the day I left at the age of eighteen. The same fields and hedgelines folding into the distance. The same dish of Jodrell Bank radio telescope on the far rim of the horizon, which I used to stare at through binoculars, feasting on its futuristic weirdness. Outside the windows, the soul of the place still waited. That's what I hoped to see.

On the programme, Second Edgecrofter Ian said: 'We bought the house because it had the best view in England.'

My parents used to say exactly this. It has the best view in England. You silly sausages, I used to think, going on about the marvellous view. Now, I thought, with almost unbearable eagerness: this will be the moment.

It wasn't the moment. Instead of looking out of the window, we went inwards for the money shots. We toured the bedrooms, master dressing room, handbags room, shoe room, Choo room, the spa with indoor infinity pool and three waterfalls. And then, in the guest suite, the presenter gasped and pointed outside.

I leaned hard into the screen. Let me see out of that window. Then I'll know where I am.

No, it was two bronze wildebeest on the lawn.

Even so, beyond the wildebeest, our view should be out there, the best view in England. When we lived at Edge Croft, you couldn't avoid the view. It was visible from every back window. Now, though, all we could see was a hedge. Where had the view gone?

We had a hedge in our day. It was about ten feet tall, but we could see over it easily because the garden sloped. Had the hedge grown to block the view? I don't think that's horticulturally possible. It would have to be fifty feet high.

Note for returning time traveller: you will grow and shrink in disorientating mind-games.

Next we went to the garage. The garage was under the house and it had mirrors. Think of a wardrobe for Ferraris. 'We had twenty cars in here one night,' said Ian. 'This is under the garden, by the way. We excavated several thousand tonnes of earth.'

That explained why we couldn't see the view. The garden, in our day, was a set of landscaped hills and the house sat at the top. That was why we could see over the hedge. When Irene and Ian rebuilt, they must have had to keep the original roof height, so they gouged out the entire site to create a car park in the basement. The kind of earthworks you'd do to build a shopping centre. (I keep thinking of shopping centres.)

Dear time traveller, you thought you were on the same ground. You are not. The ground has all gone. And with it has gone the archaeology from your years, the small stuff that survives even the most drastic rebuild. Action Man boots lost in the sandpit. Pieces of lawnmower cable. Your grey cat who lay in state on a candlelit altar in one of the outhouses before the burial ceremony in the front garden. The deposits from the family who came after you too. None of that's there now. It's all dug out like a cancer. Yes, that is melodramatic, but the scale of erasement requires it. You were there, for many important years, and you have left no trace.

We were not on the same ground.

But was it still the same sky, over the same landscape? The footpath in a crease across the field, the ponds that dried to hard-baked bowls in the drought of 1976? The curve of the road in the far distance, invisible until sundown, when it appears in a moving glitter of headlights? The blue layers of boundaries after that? And that radio telescope?

Surely Sally Lindsay would gasp if she saw that.

But nobody looked that way. It wasn't of interest to the programme. It didn't have a price tag.

The new Edgecrofters went shopping. To look at jewellery that cost more than a car, and a car that cost more than a house. A chef came to cater a dinner party with Wagyu beef steaks, which he explained would cost £120 each in a restaurant. His tone was apologetic as if he knew this was hard to understand. A troupe of croupiers arrived after dinner and set up a casino in the basement.

Dear time traveller, the future will be incomprehensibly opulent and expensive. You will feel like a bumpkin and their customs will baffle you.

I talked to my brother about it. 'It's so sad,' he said, 'that this is what Alderley Edge has become. I'm glad I knew it when it was a normal place. Well-to-do, yes, but normal.'

Some times were better-to-do than others, I remember. In the later years, we couldn't afford to fix the leaks in the roof or run the boiler.

Dear time traveller, you came for something familiar, but it has all changed too much.

Everything has gone. Except. If you look at an aerial view, the old Edge Croft is still in the roof line of the new one and in the shapes of the gables. And I began to notice the old house is also in the positioning of certain rooms. When the dinner guests of the new Edgecrofters chatted on the terrace, time ran backwards. Their terrace is perched up on a balcony because the ground is now lower, but if you measure from the centre of the Earth, that puts it in the same spot as ours was. In the 1970s, we sat in that same patch of air, drinking tea or orange squash or wine, looking out over the view, exactly as the new Edgecrofters were now.

Then in the master bedroom, a fleeting moment showed, at last, the elusive view. I knew it instantly. It was the view from my mother's bedroom. They were, they are, in the same spaces we lived in, using them for the same human purposes.

Dear time traveller, every trace of you has gone, every crumb of brick and scrap of earth. But when the new people sit on their terrace and dream into the distance, or wend their way to bed, they tread in the ghosts of your rooms.

After Us

We're in 2022 again.

'Have you found a house yet?' says Calvin.

We haven't, and not for lack of trying. Even the Chandeliers House has gone quiet.

'You could exchange with a long completion date and...'

Anything else, Calvin?

'Mick and Steph want to come round,' he says.

Why? Are they going to find faults and reduce their offer?

Still, we can't refuse them. We wait outside in the car.

After a while, the three come out, all smiles. Mick and Steph drive away. Calvin lingers at the front door. All seems well.

'They wanted to measure,' he says. 'They have exciting plans. They want to knock the kitchen and living room together to make a very big space. They want to install a bathroom with skylights in the attic.'

Later, back in possession, I find a splosh of coffee at the entrance to the attic, on the white-painted floorboards. Floorboards I painted when we did our own renovations. They spilled coffee here and they didn't even notice. In their minds, this house is already theirs.

After a while the lights came out, all except Max and Glenn dozed away. Calvin lingered at the front door. All seemed well.

They started to measure the room. They have exciting at me. They wanted to knock the kitchen and living room together to make a vast open space. There was to be a bathroom with easy access to the little patio, and in the spare room I had a splash of color on the partition to the attic, on the white painted baseboards. Floorboards. I paused when we did our own renovations. They sighed and said how much they didn't even notice. In fact, about this house's already old era.

The Searchers

The Aardvark House

A call from Liz, the Chandeliers House estate agent.

'We nearly have a deal. We are so close.'

Are we? We made an offer on the Chandeliers House several weeks ago and heard nothing.

'You could move in in five weeks. Just try a little higher.'

Five weeks? I doubt that. But it's a good house with good spaces. It's much better built than many we've seen. It's twenty minutes from my beloved stables and has heathland nearby that we could walk to. The universe is speaking. You want a house? Stop wasting time. That's the one. Don't you see? What is wrong with you?

We inch the offer up fractionally. By a toe.

Silence. Oh well, we weren't in love with it.

We look around another house. A house that pushes buttons the Chandeliers House can never reach.

It's a new-build, but not like other new-builds we've seen, which are styled in grey-beige with identical bathrooms and kitchens, as if by a standard house doctor algorithm. After a few you can't remember which is which.

This house has character. It has a New England clapboard look, welcoming and tranquil like a country railway station, with deep windows that will fill the rooms with sunshine. The garden is too big for us, but all gardens are. We could let part of it go to meadow, indeed that will definitely happen. It has a fountain that's turned on by remote control. Imagine the fun if that goes wrong. And the fun of the water bill. We don't have to use the fountain.

It's a good house. We drive home, discussing what to check before we offer. A call from the estate agent: the house is sold. Game over.

'How do people make a decision so fast?' says Dave.

'We need to offer while we're in there,' I say. 'Next time, I'll give you a codeword if I'm happy with it.'

He looks dubious.

'It's the only way. Or someone will beat us to it.'

'I suppose there's still the Chandeliers House.'

But we are not cheered. The New England house has better light than the Chandeliers House.

On Rightmove that evening, Dave finds another new-build. It has no beige at all. It's black trendy window frames, lots of glass, light from above in two places (not just one), black marble in the kitchen and bathrooms. It has a tiny garden that is a big Yes for us and surely a No for everyone else. Our fickle hearts are once again on fire. It's a ten-minute drive from the woods where we walk and ride. But there's one problem.

'Darling, it's several legs over our budget.'

'We might be able to make an offer.'

'We can't offer several legs lower.'

'Perhaps we can offer in the middle. And as it's a new build, it'll be cheaper to run than an older house and won't need the kind of maintenance, so we won't have to keep money in reserve for repairs and upkeep. Let's view it.'

The date we view the house is my birthday. I am silly about birthdays. This house will either be specially perfect or specially bad.

No, it's perfect. One particular detail has us gasping. In the kitchen, the estate agent says 'I'm going to show you the utility room,' and opens a tall pair of doors. We thought they were a cabinet. They're a concealed entrance to the utility room. It's like entering the TARDIS.

I mutter a word to Dave: 'aardvark'. We haven't agreed what the codeword will be, so I give him A Look.

He understands. I wouldn't say 'aardvark' without a good reason.

He makes an offer. It's nearly two cheeky legs below asking price, but the estate agent doesn't shoot us or turn a furious colour. She says she'll take it to the seller.

We continue with my birthday. A trip around a 15th-century stately home. We joke that we won't be making an offer. This is how we regard all houses now, as available to us. We visit friends and take them a salted caramel cake. Dave shows them the estate agent's leaflet. Don't, I say, but it's my birthday and we are allowed to be reckless with fate. The friends swoon and say things to keep the fantasy going.

The estate agent calls. We hold our breath. Offer rejected. No surprise. Ah well, we still have the Chandeliers House. We will always have the Chandeliers House, and it, apparently, will always have us. Let the birthday continue.

The next day, Dave calls the Aardvark House estate agent. What if we increased our offer a little? Too late. It's gone.

'Never mind,' I say.

'But this is the house you most liked,' says Dave. 'I didn't need the codeword. I could tell.'

A few days later, friends invite us to meet them in town. They are mysterious about the reason, then they walk us to the local register office. After thirty-three years together they are getting married, on the spur of the moment this afternoon, and we are their witnesses. A surprise wedding. It's like a surprise party, but much better.

Next day, hungover in postnuptial bonhomie and a sense that the world is full of splendid love, we get a call. Aardvark is back on the market. We repeat our offer. It's accepted.

I am so happy I cannot speak. I go for a run to let off the steam. We've found it at last, and it's the prince of houses. I jog my route and say goodbye, endless pavement. I pause at the top of a hill, study the view. Goodbye vista of roofs and blocks. Goodbye, brown tiled underpass and forests of traffic lights. Goodbye city graveyard between the railway line and supermarket. Goodbye, daily drive to escape to woods and horses. We will soon not need to escape. We'll already be there.

Proceedings start. What a relief to not be searching. This is the best house ever. All previous houses have taught us that. There was a reason we didn't get them, so we'd know Mr Right. We're not cursed after all.

Friends in Zoom calls and emails are eager to see the online listing. We don't send it. Something is sure to go wrong. But if they visit us in person, the beautiful brochure is on the kitchen table and Dave can't resist showing it off. I wince. Fate is listening.

Calvin is blowing fuses with joy. I'm sure he's about to send flowers.

Just as we're celebrating the finish line, we realise there's a problem with Aardvark. It has two oak trees very close to the walls. Many years ago, our current house developed cracks from a neighbour's tree roots.

I go to Google. Can oak trees cause subsidence? Oh my ears and whiskers, oak trees are the worst for this.

The roots of an oak are massive, bigger than the tree canopy. The two oaks at Aardvark loom over the whole roof. Now imagine that much rootage under the walls and floors. Aardvark isn't constructed on solid ground. It's resting on a cradle of tree roots that are swelling and growing all the time.

'But Aardvark is a modern build,' says Dave. 'Surely the foundations can cope.'

Yes, surely. When we built our extension, which was near the troublesome trees, the engineer specified pilings as tall as the entire house. Our walls have never since cracked.

Then we remember Aardvark had a previous offer, which disappeared in just a few days. Was that because of the oak trees?

Dave phones a surveyor.

It is not as simple as that.

'The trouble is,' says the surveyor, 'it's a new build. My survey won't show structural problems because they won't emerge for a few years. The best I can do is a snagging survey for obvious problems. And I can examine the plans.'

'Great, surely the plans will tell you everything about the structure.'

The sound of teeth sucking. 'I can't tell if what's on the plans is what was actually built under the house.'

Wouldn't that be checked? What about building inspections? When we built our extension, we had to pass numerous inspections.

'Those inspections are paid for by the builder just

to get a certificate from the council,' says the surveyor. 'They aren't a proper survey to check what was actually built.'

Then why do those inspections at all?

'Quite,' says the surveyor, which isn't much help.

I can't accept there is no information about this house's structure. I find Aardvark's planning documents on the council website and am quietly proud of myself, but they don't mention special foundations. I don't know what I'm looking at, of course, but I see nothing like the works we have under our house and our trees were saplings. But I find a letter of protest from a neighbour of Aardvark, who expresses surprise that it wasn't designed with deep pilings. Is that neighbour objecting from actual knowledge or because he's a grumbling nimby?

'Before we decide anything, let's get the surveyor's report,' Dave says. He doesn't want to give up.

We drive to our solicitor to sign some papers for when it's time to exchange contracts. The solicitor is in Woking, near the Chandeliers House. As we arrive in the town, we get a call. It's Liz, the estate agent for the Chandeliers House. She must have a Morris detector.

Our latest offer is still ongoing, it seems. Does that make us feel better?

It doesn't. Like any fallback, if it disappears, you fret. Otherwise the strongest feeling you can muster is a lukewarm shrug. We prefer Aardvark.

We get the Aardvark survey. The surveyor is

noncommittal about the foundations. He's surprised they aren't piled, but so is every armchair expert, including us. He can't say if they'll be adequate. He finds the roof has already had repairs and it's not even a year old. The big skylights will leak in ten years because they have been cheaply finished. Not good. What other cheapassery is concealed by those sleek finishes? What about the places no one can check? We thought Aardvark would be well made.

We still like it but now it's not worth the higher price. We reduce our offer. It's rejected.

I sit at my PC refreshing the Rightmove page, waiting to see Aardvark relist and drift away for ever.

I remember my jubilant run, saying goodbye to the streets. I haven't run that route since.

I want a house in a place that will give us joy, not a house in a place we need to escape from.

We trawl Rightmove several times an hour. We leap on emails from estate agents.

We bicker and grumble. I'm drawn to bungalows that have been extended into the roof with vaulted rooms and galleried spaces. They look interesting to me. Dave says: 'That's just a bungalow.'

'It's not a bungalow any more. Okay, what about this?'

'That one will be dark.'

'How can we tell if we don't stand in its rooms?'

'It faces the wrong way. Look. There's north.'

'Don't "north" me. You know I don't understand north.'

Another house I nominate is 'too small upstairs, look at the measurements on the floorplan'.

I don't speak north and I don't speak numbers. Dave paces out the numbers, showing me what a room of those dimensions would be like.

'Okay, what about this? It's big, with lots of light, recently built.'

'That road is horrible. It was on my bus route to school. But let's go and see this one.'

Now I'm the one curling my lip. 'It's very ordinary, isn't it?'

House Of Hiraeth

On the radio, two women with forceful Welsh accents are discussing a nostalgic yearning for their homeland. It's a trait of the Welsh, apparently.

Their language has a word for it: hiraeth.

'Hiraeth,' they coo, warming into its cadence, its middle R that allows you to weight the second syllable as much as the first, its satisfying growly music in the mouth, its earnestness. They are also laughing at themselves.

It is the word I need today.

I have hiraeth, in all its solemn silliness. I have it for a house I haven't stepped inside. I have only seen pictures, but they have done for me.

It's on the Hog's Back, an ancient road high on the downs in Surrey with views over a plunging valley. The estate agent's picture shows a smallish brick house with oversized windows at the top of a landscaped hill. A long set of steps leads from the terrace down the hill. When I say long, take what you're imagining and double it. Then do that again. It's at least as long as the escalator in one of our deepest London Tube stations. Think of Powell & Pressburger's *A Matter of Life and Death*.

I like that improbable mismatch of scale.

The steps lead to a lower lawn and then down again to another lawn with a small, stone-lined pond.

Somehow, the pond looks much older than the house. So does the long, long, long set of steps. I like this too.

The whole picture, the tension between giantness and tininess, intrigues me. If the garden was a teapot, the house perches at the top like a very small lid. No, like the very small knob on a very small lid.

The house itself is not handsome, at least on the outside.

'It's an ugly blot,' says Dave.

But we can forgive ugliness. If you're inside, you can't see the outside.

'And the kitchen will be dark,' he says. 'It faces north.' But he doesn't reject it, like many others.

I arrange the viewing, get more details. Its full

name and postcode so I can look up its energy documents, recent planning applications and alterations, to see if there are restrictions that might stop us changing things we don't like. We're savvy about this now.

Dave says: 'What year was it built?'

I know what he's saying. We've favoured houses built in the last ten years, for maximum heat efficiency and minimal age-related problems. And because the Chandeliers House is less than ten years old.

Such is the nature of fallbacks. The fallback becomes the baseline. Everything else must do better.

This house looks like 1950s or 60s. Quite ordinary. No period features.

Its energy documents reveal it has oil-fired heating. This is a thing we swore was a deal-breaker. Dave's disgust level rises.

Mine doesn't.

This is not like me.

Surely we simply replace the boiler with one that runs on mains gas. That must be possible.

To prove it, I find the energy certificates for other houses nearby. Do they heat with gas?

They don't. That means there's no gas main on that high, ancient road.

The broadband is good, though. That's often a worry with old roads.

Okay, the oil-fired boiler might have to be replaced with something super-advanced like a ground source heat pump. You can get grants for those, can't you?

I have no idea whether you can or can't. But something keeps me opening the house's page and touring again through the rooms.

You'll know when you've found The One, a friend says to me. And this house feels known, like something from an old dream. Its perched view, with the massively cascading lawn down a long valley, with fields at the bottom. The 1960s windows.

It's Edge Croft, the way I knew it. The way my parents rejigged it with lots of glass to let the view in. Which I thought made it look like a bus garage, but never mind.

Househunting is archaeological excavation. Not just of houses but of the self. I already belong there. Hiraeth.

I want to know everything about the house. I read the estate agent description. I see a detail that I previously missed and my heart sings hallelujah. The house was built on the site of a Victorian mansion.

I knew it. This is why it looks so charmingly dwarfed, like a small person on an operatic stage.

Its name is Great Down. I type this into Google.

Oh heavens. Great Down is the name of the original mansion, which was demolished in the 1950s. I find a postcard of it from 1906. It was celebrated enough for postcards to be made, like Manderley in *Rebecca*. There it is, on the cascaded mound that intrigues me so, and filling every inch of its width. A building that looks as long as an ocean liner, curved at its grand end. A forest of chimneys, a handsome line of windows edged with pale stone. Glamorous things might have happened behind those windows; weekend parties with gleaming silver and long-stemmed glasses and whirling dresses in a ballroom. It is a place that deserves stories, like Downton Abbey and Brideshead. And Manderley.

And yes, the long set of garden steps in the picture is the same set of steps that is there today. The steps now lead to the quiet house that stands on the footprint of those big lives. The terrace, which has a stone wall with ornamental edging like plaited pastry, is — it really is — the same terrace that's shown in the 1906 pictures. The first people who stood there had stepped out of the grand old house. The old house is still in the footings. Still in the name.

Dave sends me the nightly crop of houses we might seriously consider. They are sensible but soulless. My dance card is marked by Great Down.

We will look at it on Monday. When we go there, maybe I'll come to my senses. Maybe I won't. We will probably argue about it.

'I really want to give this house a proper chance,' I say to Dave.

When we drive to view it, I worry that I'm dragging him there unwillingly. But he seems eager, as though we're setting out on an adventure. He is giving it a chance.

We arrive early and scout the area. I have already researched this, to see what it will be like for Dave, who does not drive. Is there a pavement so he can walk to footpaths, stations and bus stops? There is. I've seen it on Google Streetview. Are there bus stops?

That's complicated.

The Hog's Back is a dual carriageway, and a very fast one. We know it well by car. We've driven it countless times. If your house is on it, you can only exit in one direction, to the left. That requires gravel-spitting acceleration because the traffic is at motorway speeds. You wait for a gap then surge out, praying. If you want the other way, you drive to the crossing spot, stop, wait for a gap and make a second surge.

That's not so bad. I could get used to it. But Dave might need to cross that road on foot to catch a bus. If he wanted to travel to Farnham he'd be on the correct side for the number sixty-five. If he wanted to come back, he'd risk becoming roadkill. Cars on this road do not expect to see pedestrians. There are no crossings with lights. Indeed there is a hazard sign that warns you to look out for people making a desperate dash. We have cackled at this whenever we've whizzed past. What kamikaze person would try to cross this road?

I've looked at the Ordnance Survey, hoping for footpaths. Perhaps an underpass. Surely people sometimes walk here.

There's nothing. If you don't drive, you don't go anywhere.

We arrive early to recce. The maps might have missed something. We park in the nearby village, take a walk up a wooded path that leads to the dual carriageway and the traffic at blur speed. I've seen this already from my Streetview explorations. I know that the house is a short walk from this footpath, and if you come this way there's a pavement to deliver you safely.

We are close to it. Its territory begins just the other side of the hedge. I feel a shiver.

Walking back to the car, a chap in a BT van asks if we need directions. 'Because nobody ever uses that path,' he says. Dave has the grace to look surprised at this.

Time to drive to the house. Because of the dual carriageway this requires a detour around the bottom of the hill and through another village to approach from the correct side, which takes about ten minutes even though we could just walk up the path and around the hedge.

We turn into the gateway. We see another house, a dinky cottage with latticed windows surrounded by stone. From its style, it looks like an appetiser for the old mansion. The name confirms it: Great Down Lodge. It's the gatehouse for the original house. Carved into the plasterwork is a date: 1873. I gasp. The earliest date I've seen for Great Down is 1906, but 1873 must be the actual build date. Its story is older than I thought, by several decades. Its glamour quotient rises. With so much of it erased, these details seem talismanic.

I bombard Dave with these observations. He is being notably patient.

We tour the house. I have déjà-vu, wall to wall. So many details are Edge Croft, and not just the setting.

The bedroom balcony has square concrete tiles, wired glass and a wooden handrail. This combination is not at all lovely, and was probably put in thousands of houses, but it is exactly what we had at Edge Croft and I have not seen it elsewhere until this moment.

The heavens open. Thick rain lashes the windows. Another piece of Edge Croft comes back; savage hilltop weather. I know how cold it will get here.

We splash out into the garden. Dave and the estate agent flee back indoors again. I stay out and venture further, descend the steps down the cascading lawns, which takes some time, all the way down, getting soaked. At the bottom, I turn to look up. I have a photo of Edge Croft just like this, a wall of windows far up high, reflecting the sky, inscrutable as a face behind sunglasses. Here at Great Down, this hill is even steeper and longer, the reversed telescope of memory. I'm looking at a place that seems to know things I want to know. One vanished house on top of another.

I run back up the steps that survive intact from the old house. I walk on the terrace. I am grateful to the people who left these here, didn't destroy them. I walk and look, and imagine doing this much more slowly, learning every shape and crack, with all the time in the world, instead of the brief minutes we have here today. I imagine sitting on quiet nights with ghosts circulating out of the postcard of 1906. I imagine looking out over the valley, learning it too as it changes with the ongoing seasons. I imagine sharing all this with the people we will bring here.

Time's up. We leave in the rain, do the brave surge into the traffic and the second brave surge to change direction.

'I would love this to be our house,' I say. 'But there are too many awkward things.'

Dave doesn't say I told you so. He knew from the start and let me take my time.

'I wonder what's on Rightmove tonight?' I say.

Dave's mobile rings. 'That'll be Liz about the Chandeliers House,' he says.

Instead of saying 'hello Liz', he says 'hello Penny'.

Penny is the agent for the Aardvark House.

What's happening? I try to drive quietly so I can decipher the faint squawking of her words.

'No,' says Dave. 'We'd definitely want that. But thanks. Bye.'

Is Aardvark back in play?

'The seller has made a counter-offer. A bit higher than our latest offer. But they'll give us £10k off if we do without the house-builder's guarantee.'

We can't do without the guarantee. That's one of the reasons to get a new house. The surveyor warned us to check any problems would be under warranty. Leaky roofs and all that.

'If we'd known they were slapdash, we wouldn't have aardvarked it,' says Dave. Aardvarked is our new verb.

We drive on, through the rain. We discuss. Aardvark has been on the open market but they've come back to us. That means there are no other offers.

This means we shouldn't increase ours, we should stick. Because they want the deal.

And what about the oak trees and the foundations? No one seems to know if they'll be trouble or not. They could be uncontrollably expensive. Actually, why haven't the sellers got the guarantee already? That's a whole separate discussion.

There is still the Chandeliers House. It's also new, but not so new that a survey would be meaningless. And it's being lived in by the bloke who built it, so it must be habitable.

The reclusive seller of the Chandeliers House is still thinking.

*Summoned By The
Chandeliers Recluse*

On a Friday afternoon, we are driving through Woking and our Toyota is telling us to 'tit' again. It must also have put up the Bat Signal because Liz phones about the Chandeliers House.

'No,' says Dave, 'we haven't found anywhere else yet.'

Sometimes we imagine ourselves in the Chandeliers House. It seems a very possible future. This is one of those times. Is that only because we haven't found anything better? If the house knew this, it would give us a talking-to. I'm not your consolation prize. You don't totally want me. Or do you? Make up your mind because I won't wait for ever.

Now Liz says: 'The seller wants to meet you.'

We've met him fleetingly on previous visits. When we say hello, his eyes slide sideways as though he thinks it's a trick question. He is always dressed in the same outfit; jeans and a navy blue Ralph Lauren zip fleece, so unvarying it's like a factory setting, and not what I'd expect of a man so fond of chandeliers.

He's always preferred to hide, but now he has asked to meet us. Whatever for?

'I don't know why he wants to meet you,' says Liz. 'But a previous offer fell through with no explanation so he wants to talk to you.'

Do we have to pass a test and prove we truly want the house? I know that might be stretching the comparison with romcoms, but we can't imagine what he wants.

'I'll be there too,' says Liz.

We're grateful for that.

We arrive at the Chandeliers House. Liz shows us into the kitchen. The seller is called Tom. He's standing at the marble worktop, bent over and looking intently at his hands.

We say hello. He doesn't speak or look up. He remains exactly where he is.

Did he really ask to meet us?

Liz puts on a breezy smile. 'So,' she says, 'this is to discuss the extras, which Tom will include with the house for another...' She names a sum. On our scale of the price as a human figure, it's most of another leg. She chuckles. 'The chandeliers alone are at least an arm.'

I know what Dave's thinking, and it's the same as me. We never wanted the chandeliers anyway. We're not about to pay extra for them.

More to the point, why are we talking about extras? Aren't they agreed later with the contracts? And in the privacy of an email, not in a meeting where you tell the seller 'no we don't want that stuff', to their face?

Although Tom isn't letting us see his face. I'm reminded of a resentful child who has been dragged to say hello to visitors and has decided he will punish everyone.

It's clear what's going on. They want to embarrass us into increasing our offer.

Liz picks up a sheaf of papers. 'Let's go round with the list.' She sets off into the hall with brisk cheeriness, as though she's confident she'll persuade us to splurge a little and treat ourselves.

Of course that's not happening. We say no to the three-storey glass-spear chandelier in the stairwell. No to the Titanic teleport chandelier in the dining room.

'So Tom will replace those with ordinary light fittings,' says Liz, a little sternly. 'Is that what you want?'

'Totally happy with that,' we say.

Tom himself is still in the kitchen, keeping away.

Liz continues to the bathrooms. We're asked to

consider the mirrors. They have lights that change colour through blue, violet, orange, green and red. No to those. We'd have got rid of them. How often would we want a disco in the bathroom?

Liz reads the next item on the list. 'The shutters on the windows.' Her voice rises to a surprised squeak. This is too much, even for her. She calls out. 'Tom, the shutters? You can't take the shutters to another house, can you? What would you do with them?'

Dave and I reply in chorus. 'We don't need the shutters.' And we don't. We were going to remove them. They make the rooms dark.

Liz takes us back to the kitchen. Tom is still studying his hands in thick, sulking silence.

'So,' says Liz, 'the curtains in here are on the list.'

No. We don't want curtains in the kitchen. Who does?

Tom has not spoken or moved. Liz looks ready to tell us all to stop being impossible. But we haven't failed to grasp the agenda here; we just don't want any of these fittings. And if Tom didn't want to hear this, he shouldn't have asked for a meeting.

Now what?

I had been curious to meet Tom. He built the house and I wanted to talk about that. I wanted to hear about the choices he made. They're part of the house's story. I ask about the name. 'Why did you call it Pembroke? Is that name personal for you?'

Tom doesn't answer. The silence continues for a long time. Liz revives like the trouper she is. 'The name

Summoned By The Chandeliers Recluse

of the house, Tom,' she says, as though he hasn't realised he's been spoken to. 'They want to know how you chose the name of the house.'

Tom speaks. 'It was the name of the house that was on the site before.' He says this to his hands. If this conversation had footnotes to explain the characters' true thoughts, they would be unprintable.

I try again, because we would like to buy this house if the price was sensible. 'Tom, this shade of white you've used on the walls. It's a nice choice. Not too stark, not too grey. What is it?'

Silence. Liz says: 'The paint colour, Tom.'

'It's diamond white,' says Tom, and unprintables appear in the footnotes again.

The only thing to do is look at our watches and say 'hey ho, must get on, nice meeting you, cheerio'.

Later, Liz calls. 'Terribly sorry about that. You were coming from a position of positivity and he was coming from a position of negativity and hopefully we can all meet in the middle.'

'You did your best,' we say, while sprinting through the day's new offerings on Rightmove.

Calvin phones, and catches us in a rare moment when we have real news.

'We've made an offer, but the seller has put his price up considerably.'

'I think,' Calvin replies, 'that you'll find it worthwhile to pay that extra leg.'

How silly of us. We still think of an extra leg as actual pounds from a bank account.

We wonder what would happen if we asked Mick and Steph for another leg. Calvin could tell them it would be worth their while.

A few days later, Liz calls again. An offer from Tom. Pay just a bit more, not even as much as an arm, and he'll throw in all the extras.

But we don't want the extras. Not any of them. He can sell them to someone else and we'll keep the money for other things. What about our offer?

Silence.

The Show Must Go On And On

In case you're wondering about Mick and Steph, they're still pushing to exchange. Calvin pursues this tirelessly. They're renting. We could rent too while we look. We refuse tirelessly. We'll exchange when we know we can exchange on a place ourselves. In a chain. Doesn't anyone do that any more?

We keep Calvin supplied with a lively selection of news. It's like the days when I worked on a news magazine and we had to find stories to fill the pages. We made two offers this week. We're lining up another. We're arranging a survey, hooray.

In real life, our options are fizzling away. Aardvark isn't yet abandoned, but it's now highly doubtful because of its issues and price.

We don't tell Calvin this. We tell him we have a plan B, which is the Chandeliers House.

Only now it's not. I've just spotted the Chandeliers House on Rightmove at last, for the high price we can't meet. Now it's sure to get offers. Our refusal to also buy the chandeliers, disco mirrors, shutters and kitchen curtains was finally curtains for us. Tom has at last allowed Liz to put pictures of it online. That's how much we offended him.

After Liz's fervent chasing of us, and our chasing of Liz and the house, we feel betrayed, but I guess that's business.

Mick and Steph visit our house again, bringing an eco-consultant. We vacate while they wander within. It's a sweltering day, lovely for sitting in the garden, but the thing we most want to talk about is how our plans are collapsing, so we climb into the car to make sure we're not overheard. We sit wilting in its superheated sauna interior.

After a while, Mick and Steph come out. We emerge, like hot lettuce, say hello. There is buoyant chit-chat, and no one would think we ever get frustrated with each other.

I look at their smiling faces, full of plans. Those smiles would turn savage if we told them how our move looks now.

Calvin hangs back as we wave them off.

The Show Must Go On And On And On

'What have you got planned for the weekend?' he says.

It's Wednesday. I can't think of words about weekends.

Dave is better at conversation than I am. 'We went to a couple of friends' housewarmings recently.'

Well played, Dave. Make him believe that's all we think about.

'You'll be having your own housewarming soon,' says Calvin.

I manage a bright, believer smile, but we will not be having a housewarming soon, because there is no house to buy, and this is all about to crash.

Coming And Going

Where You Belong

I have a friend who has lived in the same street in a Surrey village for his whole life. When he left his childhood home he didn't go very far. He bought a house a few doors away and that's where he brought up his own family. He is deeply embedded in the place and has celebrated this attachment in many novels. There is now a street named after him, to his slight embarrassment. This village is his centre of gravity, where he has always happily belonged.

My father searched a long time for a place where he belonged. He didn't feel at home at home. He didn't sleep well there.

Nor did he sleep well in hotels or in other people's houses.

There were just a few places in the world where he could get a good night's sleep.

One of those places was Vienna. He liked its grace and heritage, and especially the Habsburg royal family. He memorised their family tree, the details of who shot who, who succeeded who, who married their own sister, who had haemophilia, who went mad. My brother and I endured long lectures that were very confusing.

My father hinted that he hoped he also had secret blue blood. He loved fine palaces and royal uniforms. Could that be a race memory? He believed such things were seeded in the blood. Whenever he went to Vienna, he slept well.

The other place he slept well was a village in Scotland. In his quest to find a distinguished ancestor, he researched Winnie, his mother, who died in the sanatorium near my house in London. Winnie was born with the surname Laurie. My father found a Laurie family connected with a stately home in Dumfriesshire and travelled up there to investigate.

He phoned from the hotel on the first night, brimming with discoveries.

'I was sitting in the pub, minding my own business, and a lady kept chatting to me, asking me what I was doing here. I didn't want to tell her the real reason, so I said I was on holiday, but she kept on so eventually I said I'm here to research a family connection. And she said "I knew it! I knew you were one of them. You have their ways".'

She could not have made him happier. Whether he had their ways or not, there were drinks all round, and all became happier still.

Father returned home a few days later. He'd been to the Lauries' ancestral mansion, Maxwelton, which was in the Laurie family from 1611 to 1968, until death duties forced them to sell. The new owners, the Stenhouses, had opened it to the public. They showed him around, especially the gift shop. Father now drew from his bag a privately produced book about the Laurie family and a box of Maxwelton postcards.

Ah, we said. They sold you the relatives kit.

Teasing aside, we could see this mattered. At last he was connected with something aristocratic, even if it wasn't as gilded as the Habsburgs. This seemed to be the most important thing that had ever happened to him. I embraced it too, with eight-year-old solemnity, because it made me an interesting person with a stately home in my DNA. There were also baronets, or were they barons? I was unsure of the difference. But we now had a distinguished heritage and I looked forward to using it.

This required some preparation. Nobody knew of the Lauries. I would have to explain. I only knew one notable Laurie fact. A song, 'Annie Laurie'.

You might ask, what song 'Annie Laurie'?

Never mind. Most people didn't know 'Annie Laurie' and that was fortunate, because I had to learn it for piano lessons and it's a sappy dirge about Annie, who is bonny and gets engaged to be married. Goody gumdrops, that doesn't impress an eight-year-old.

I inspected the family tree in the Lauries book. I noted we were not on it. Neither were any of our known relatives. Was it really us?

Of course it's us, retorted my father. He trampled all objections with relentless lists. Who married who. He should have been a barrister. He persisted until I was so confused I had to agree, to make him stop. There were no shootings or haemophilia, by the way.

And therein lay another problem. I wanted to play along but the Lauries seemed dull. I couldn't get enthused about baronets and a line of lords. Or Annie of the song. But as I scoured the family tree I found someone. 'John Laurie, Shakespearean actor.'

John Laurie. Shakespearean actor. That's what it said. I knew of the BBC sitcom actor John Laurie who played Private Frazer in *Dad's Army*. Every episode had a set-piece moment where he rolled his eyes and intoned 'We're doomed', like the tolling of a great Scots bell. That John Laurie? Yes it was, for here was a picture in the book, glaring eyeballs and swooping brows. Maybe he'd been famous for Shakespeare a long time before.

But this was a cheering discovery. One of the Lauries was an actor. That was something I could admire. And John Laurie the actor did look like my father and uncle, but maybe all men do when they start to lose their hair.

As my father lined up his Laurie baronets and took them into his self-story, I informed classmates with great seriousness that I was related to a classical thesp. That's what the official book said; never mind *Dad's Army*.

We internalised our Laurieness, my father and I. I had little occasion to use it, but it had been embedded and reinforced at a young age like a religion, and so in my twenties I told Dave: 'I'm related to a Shakespearean actor.'

Wow, he said. 'Gielgud? Olivier?'

When I told him, there was an outburst of choking and eye-wiping. I'm still embarrassed by it. He's still amused and mentions it from time to time, just because of the surprise. It is the only thing Dave ever teases me about, the earnestness with which I delivered this news. Another friend who was present at the time refers to me affectionately as Roz WD WD Morris, which means Roz 'We're-Doomed-We're-Doomed' Morris.

And goodness, it shows I needed to find my own rewarding achievements, instead of borrowing someone else's.

My father visited Maxwelton at least once a year. He sent postcards of Maxwelton House in its estate of manicured parkland, of the private chapel decorated with coats of arms, of the grand hall with baronial panelling. What thoughts did he have as he wandered those places now, listening for race memories? When he was a child in the 1930s, Lauries were still living here and had been for more than 300 years. Lauries were still here until 1968, by which time my brother and I had been born.

My father always reported that he'd had, at Maxwelton, the best night's sleep for months. He always called on the Stenhouses to chat about the Lauries. On one postcard he admitted he might have overstepped for they gently told him: 'We think of this as the Stenhouse home now'.

In the cold light of day, how close is that family connection? We're not on the family tree and Google tells me that Laurie is the most common surname in Scotland. More common than Smith. As the years pass, the link with the high folk of Maxwelton becomes increasingly tenuous, at least to me. Now it's just a funny thing we once did.

But since my father died, I've connected with more of the men in his line. His cousins and my cousins.

Many of them I had never met, but I knew them from first glance. Now in middle to late middle age, to a man, they all have the John Laurie furious Frazer brow and glaring doomcasting eyes.

So I can say this: we certainly have their ways.

Peter Turns The Page

Today a friend is dismantling his bookshop. I'd like to be there but I have a deadline so I'm at my desk, sometimes thinking about what's going on without me.

In that bookshop I had my first signing event, my authorial coming of age. Until then, I rarely met the people who bought my books. Seven years on, the bookshop has become a home from home, as it is for most of Surrey's writers, illustrators and bookish people. All of us gathered together by Peter, a former teacher and IT something. This year, though, the shop lease is up and Peter has decided to retire.

It was happenstance that first brought me through those doors. The building was originally a bank, but one day, darn me, I saw the sign said Barton's Bookshop. I went in to browse. I wouldn't have told Peter I was an author, but I asked for books on writing craft then had to explain why I'd already read everything on his shelves.

When your next book is published, he said, come for a signing. With that I joined his author clan.

This clan is extensive. Peter thrives on signings and gatherings. He hosts an annual book festival in the shop. Some years, the trade is roaring. Some years, the weather is roaring and we sit looking pleadingly at a drenched empty high street, bonding in adversity. We console ourselves with Peter's special cake, a thickly iced chocolate fudge which he bakes for the launch parties of his favourite writers, which is all of them. Peter has a long white beard that gets him work as an extra in movies about Vikings, and he is one of the county's Santas.

The bookshop has shaped numerous destinies. Chat to any local journalist, artist, librarian, teacher or publishing pro and they once worked at Barton's on Saturdays.

So the bookshop is a legend, and the building is too. It was designed to be noticed, a tall, stripy edifice that resembles a Tudor guildhall or a mint humbug. Because it was a bank it has a strongroom with a thick iron door like a compartment in a submarine. Inside are important papers, extra stock and weird leftovers from book promotions. A giant cut-out picture of Michael Caine. Another of Ricky Gervais. In the gloom you see heads and shoulders, the Terracotta Army, in celebrities.

One day Peter says to me: 'Do you want to co-host a radio show about books and writing?' He knows some guys who've set up a radio station in the old dry-cleaning shop. They are looking for programmes.

Eek, I can't go on the radio. Talk for an hour without awkward pauses and stumblings? But Peter isn't worried, so I say yes.

It is a hoot. We make fifty-two episodes. We record in the shop. We learn not to fidget or drum our fingers because it sounds like avalanches and gunfire. We make our first episodes while the shop is open, hiding by the crime fiction shelves, for real-life background bookshop bustle, but discover our voices are too quiet. A bus passing outside drowns us completely, even though we are inches away from the mic. So does the beeping of the till at the far end of the shop, and the voice of Fran, Peter's assistant, serving customers. Fran's throat is a natural megaphone. He could teach voice projection. He and the buses are more clear on the tape than the whispery musings of bookwormy Roz and Peter. We move our recording time to a Sunday after closing, and deeper into the stacks, to the travel section, where the extra layers of books form a soundproof cave. Also, Sunday is Fran's day off.

The shop is a playground for our show. We run around pulling titles for our topic of the week. One week we discuss book covers. Book covers on the radio. There's nothing we can't do.

I write a travel memoir. One of my stories is about another bookshop, in a disused chapel full of abstract statues, where the owner, Bob, makes you tea and plays Bix Beiderbecke LPs as you browse. One day I get a phone call. It's Peter, on holiday in Suffolk with a copy of my book. He has found the chapel shop. Right now he's talking to Bob, showing him the chapter in which he features. They send me pictures, two white-haired book crusaders, surrounded by old volumes. They look like Time Lords.

And now Peter's shop is closing. He is retiring.

The loss will be felt through all the firmament. On Facebook, for instance. Peter has a tireless appetite for Facebook and his friends include people I knew pre-internet, from school and college. How has he collected them? He chats to them more often than I do. So when he announces his retirement, there is uproar. A trip to Barton's was probably on the bucket list of bookish folk all round the planet.

There is a mighty party. So many readers, authors, people who've worked there. We are finishing a life phase. We will not coincide again so easily. A card lies open on the counter. It arrived in the post from well-wishers at the Rotary Club and is not for everyone to sign now, but it is next to the wine, so everyone writes in it anyway. The cardboard celebrity army from the vault is here. The lifesize effigy of Michael Caine is taken away as a souvenir by a longtime loyal customer. Ricky Gervais, so far as I know, doesn't find a home.

After the doors close, the great dismantling begins. That's the day I'm at my desk with a deadline, checking chapter titles, writing captions and cross-references. The shop is on my mind. Who is there? I want to be there too.

Once I've finished my work, I message Peter.

'Still loads to do,' he says. 'Do come.'

I can go there one more time. It feels like a blessing.

The shelves are empty. The books that remain are in boxes. The sofas, counter, tables and racks have gone.

The main job now is removing the shelves. Another bookshop is opening nearby in the old Carphone Warehouse. They are glad to have the Bartons shelves. I help the new owner carry them up the high street. The shelf labelled crime fiction and the shelf labelled travel, where Peter and I hid to make our whispering radio show.

With this, we are removing the shop's internal structure. The shelves formed a warren of corridors and dens. It's a shell now, one big space. Possibly how it looked when it was the bank, before the bookshop. People from that time would recognise it again.

Every helper gets a souvenir. I leave with the Valentine's Day display. A champagne bucket and a fake rose. 'There's a pair of stockings somewhere that belongs with that,' says Peter, but he can't find them. Every helper also gets a special book, a hardback volume about the lost railway stations of Surrey. A crate of these has been sitting in the vault for a decade or more, left after a launch party, and not as popular as everyone hoped. The typesetting is terrible — tiny lettering over wide pages, like the small print of a contract, and the black and white photos all look roughly the same, so only diehard enthusiasts would read it.

At home, Dave and I chuckle about its dull presentation, but also decide it could be fun. We will look for these lost stations the next time we want an adventure.

The book sits on the kitchen table for a while, then moves to a mysterious other pile on its way to somewhere vague, then vanishes into the huge population of books we have in our house so now we can't find it. It has made a hiding place among other book chums, exactly as if it never left Barton's.

Proving Myself

We are visiting Dave's school for an open day. The building dates from 1586. If people of that time mentioned the English monarch they meant Elizabeth I. In Dave's school, we walk up the 1586 staircase. Its oak banisters are so soaked in polish and varnish that they have changed their nature to something eternal and mineral, like an ancient galleon.

I imagine coming in at the beginning of the school term, the smell of beeswax and great expectations. 'This must be a real timeslip for you,' I say. Not especially, says Dave, but then he comes back regularly for reunions. And to his college in Oxford, which is even older, by three Henrys, three Edwards, a Richard, a Jane and a Mary.

I have just filled in an application form for a writing job with a multinational corporation. Their vetting is exhaustive, including every official document about my education. My O and A level certificates are long lost so they want the name and address of my school. I write it on the form, but it won't be any use. The school is gone, merged with another, its site sold for demolition and the name buried. I also don't have my university degree certificate, so I fill in the name and address of my college, which has also gone, name and all. They want me to prove myself with the places that taught me about the world but now there is nothing of them.

I take a picture of Dave at the arched gateway to his school. He looks grounded and happy in a place that has always been there, has always belonged to him, and always will.

Forever And Adieu

In 1997, Anne and Steve have bought a house to restore. They are recently married and this is where they will settle.

The house will be a long haul. It's Edwardian, fallen on hard times, partitioned into bedsits with kitchens on every floor, all bashed up and studenty.

Anne is a friend from college. The college cohort is here today as she shows us round. We're now inching into grown-up roles, with job titles and business cards, spouses and cars. But not so long ago, we all arrived in one place to begin new lives, and it was a place like this.

Big rooms divided with plasterboard.

Noticeboards holed by drawing-pins. Bar heaters cemented into blocked fireplaces. That bareness is now bleak, but when we first met it was a blank slate for our new independence. We filled it with our personalities, our posters, theatre programmes, music albums, student union cards and signifiers of our new selves. There was so much to discover. Life, love, coursework, questions about what we'd turn into. Any room would do.

Anne and Steve transform the house. We return after a year and they've torn out the bedsit horrors. Found the original fireplaces and plasterwork under the partitions. We marvel — and we grow up a bit more. This might be our first house-party gathering where everyone has a proper guest room instead of crashing on the floor or sofa. Anne and Steve are showing the way to a new life stage, the houses where we will drop our deepest anchors, make families.

In the fullness of time, Steve's job relocates several hundred miles across the country.

They have to move. The house doesn't sell. I visit for Anne's birthday. They've been on the market for months and no one has made an offer. The estate agent has lost heart, and so have Anne and Steve. She mentions almost casually that buyers are coming that afternoon, the first for weeks. She is despairing that the house has anything good going for it.

I help her tidy up. I remember what she and Steve made this house from, those rabbit-hutch student digs. I remember the living-room fireplace, of brown shiny

1970s bricks like a memorial in a municipal park, which they must have had to remove with a road drill and massive courage in case it brought the whole wall down.

This noble place has had no takers? I can't accept that.

I sweep magazines into cupboards, stow baby buggies and crates of Evian in the cellar, search the kitchen cupboards for jugs to put on shelves as ornaments. I'm not like this at home. Our own house is an undesigned muddle.

Anne is a bit surprised but she can see I have a mission. Also she's so jaded I could probably put a muddy boot in every corner and she'd trust I knew what I was doing.

When the buyers arrive, she lets me show them around. I tell them all the ways the house is special, how it was restored with love, filled with years of good vibes. In an upstairs fireplace, I've placed a red curly cuddly snake, and the buyers are surely thinking it can't normally live there, but it's made them look at the grate with the Art Nouveau curves and so I can talk, one more time, about original features.

I'm going to a wedding party afterwards, so I nip up to a bathroom to change. When I come down the stairs the buyers haven't left. They are basking in the afternoon light in the hall, chatting to Anne. They spot me in my party dress and laugh. 'You didn't have to get dolled up to make us buy it.'

There is something settled and comfortable about

this tableau, as if time has paused to let us all understand. It's done. A new future for them all is taking shape.

Still Searching

X-ray Vision

Some of the houses we have viewed are on roads I travel regularly. I now pass them with new eyes. We have been into every nook and cranny, peered in bedrooms, opened cupboards, poked wherever we pleased.

House owner, your spaces are no longer private. You are on your daily doings, and we think we know where you are doing what. We have opinions, for instance about whether you wish the kitchen wasn't so dark.

Some of those houses we dearly wanted, and we see you in there a little enviously. Some we dithered about, like a coat tried on in a shop and put back on the rail because we couldn't decide. In that time, though, they belonged to us as a perhaps.

We pass you, quietly living there, with an impertinent sense of ownership, with x-ray vision.

Romcom Rules: We Can Change

Dave and I are thinking about romcoms again. Perhaps they have another lesson for us. At the start, you don't like what you'll like in the end.

Every time we step out of the car, we might find The One. We still believe that. But are we letting it find us? Or are we too fussy?

I talk to Anne. She has found several Right Ones, though one of them required much bravery.

'You'll know The One,' she says. 'Don't settle for less.'

But if a house is eighty percent or seventy percent, it can be changed. More reliably than a human can, if we're thinking in romcoms.

What about a fifty percent?

We look at a bungalow, extended with big windows and split levels, like the 2020s reinventing the 1960s. We love that. We don't love the bedrooms, which are 1960s without reinvention; small with prison-cell windows, probably the original building. The estate agent sees our discomfort and says 'you could knock those rooms together because that's not a support wall'. We discuss afterwards, as if taking the wall away is as easy as a mouse-click. We might make windows bigger too. But wait, is this house eighty percent or is it just fifty? Do we feel Anne's thunderbolt or are we trying to change ourselves to feel it?

You should use a search agent, says Calvin. Tell me what you're looking for and I'll find you one.

'A search agent?' splutters Dave. 'Is this someone else who can cream money off us?'

Still Don't Know

On the first Saturday in July, we raise our wineglasses and say: we'll know by next weekend.

We also said this last weekend.

We'll have found a perfect house, we said. A house that, right now, we haven't even met. The Chandeliers Recluse will commit or quit. Or our buyers will pull out.

This weekend, some small things have changed. The Chandeliers House has sold subject to contract. We discover this on Rightmove. We feel we should have been given a final chance after all the hard flirting. And it was hard flirting from them, not us. But it's our fault too. We never absolutely said no. A romcom lesson.

Aardvark is still in play. We still love the house, but we have to be sensible. Its unknowns could be horribly expensive. The war in Ukraine has put inflation into overdrive. As an example, the price of petrol had already reached £1.60 a litre a few months ago, which was frightening, and now it's soared to £1.90. Financially minded friends are warning it is the worst time to buy a house. Or sell one.

We call Penny, the Aardvark agent, and reduce our offer again. She says: 'I don't think they'll like it'.

In any other life situation, we'd feel bad about this. But Penny originally tried to wile us into bidding against ourselves, then to accept the house with no warranties. Looking back, how has the Aardvark relationship not disintegrated?

But it hasn't, so Dave tells Penny: 'Tell them this offer is real now but we're running out of time with our buyers.'

We thought this would be so easy. On our first outing, we found a good house on budget, won the bidding war and even avoided overbidding. A swap of paperwork and everything should have been done. But the seller pulled out and it's been impossible ever since.

We top up the wine. We imagine similar lubricated scenes in certain other houses this Saturday night. Although we haven't signed any contracts, we're in a chain. A chain of emotions. At Aardvark, they're striding the black kitchen, shouting 'No!' The

Chandeliers Recluse is rubbing his hands because he doesn't have to dignify our offers with a reply or even a thought. The only people more helpless than us are our buyers, Mick and Steph, who must be howling 'When?'

But they must be pursuing other places, like we are with Chandelier, Aardvark and anything else with walls. We're all playing the field.

Playing the field. Actually, this isn't a romcom. It's the game of homes, which is a race in which we can't see the other contestants. Or how many other contestants there really are.

Getting Hostile

Aardvark Is Back

A surprise call from Penny about Aardvark. The seller has made a low, daring offer for a house to renovate. If that goes well, he'll accept ours.

We didn't think he'd even consider. We've whittled him down by nearly three legs.

Perhaps we're turning into Mick and Steph.

We certainly are not. I have a list of reasons and circumstances to prove this. But reasons and circumstances are irrelevant. Only one thing counts — what you'll accept.

Speaking of Mick and Steph, Calvin is

away on holiday. That gives us a bit of peace.

No, he has a colleague, who calls on the dot of 10am and says 'What do I tell Mick and Steph today?'

Calvin's colleague is a chip off the old block so let's call him Alvin.

'Tell Mick and Steph it's the same as yesterday, Alvin.'

In case he doesn't know what was said yesterday, we tell him how many balls we've got in the air. Offers all over the place. We might find ourselves accepted for three houses at once. These statements are true, but they seem like fairy stories.

Why don't we stop? Because we seem so close. We have an offer for our house, which is surely the hardest part. And because of that we can find a home that isn't so ridiculously far from the woods and hills and fields that are our soul-time. There have been so many nearlys. We just have to open Rightmove and be lucky.

And suddenly, we are.

Rusty Tractor Is Back

Rusty Tractor is back on Rightmove. To remind you, this is the house we offered on in March with the hostile estate agent and the seller who jacked up the price by an arm and a leg. The house never sold after all. It's back with a new agent.

Is it worth another go? Yes, but it's a fifty percent. It has problems. Water has leaked into the main bedroom, leaving brown halos around the ceiling lights. Water and wires; an electrical timebomb? We will need advice. In another room, the light switch was taped over, a warning that it shouldn't be used. There are weird aircon units in several bedrooms, which suggest an ugly problem of some sort, perhaps with stifling heat. It might need complicated work. So when the seller hoicked his price up we ran away laughing.

But over the months as we've played with what-ifs and wine, we've discussed that house. We liked it. It has a high terrace and a view over fields with horses, and the charming rusty tractor painted like an artwork. We imagined sitting there with the sun going down, listening to the wind in the grass.

Now it's back, at its original asking price, which is affordable with the price we're getting from Mick and Steph, even with repairs. Are we getting a break at last?

Whatever, it's a new episode for Alvin.

He seems satisfied.

We call to book a viewing as soon as possible.

Buggeration. No one can see the house until the weekend, which is five days away. The estate agent wants to crowd the viewings into an open day to stir up a bidding war.

In March, we saw it at an open day and had to trick our way in. This house is still making us fight at every turn. In a romcom, that would mean we're destined for it. In real life, it's five whole days for Mick and Steph to pull the plug, which they must be busting to do.

But on Saturday, we've made it through the week and we're at the house. 'Oh,' says a cheery voice. 'I saw Morris in the list and hoped it was you. Are you still looking?'

We've seen this estate agent several times in this

mad year. She showed us the house we won that was then withdrawn from sale. And the house with enough bedrooms for the Waltons. And the house of loos with the Cold War safehouse annexe. Now here she is, MC for Rusty Tractor. We tell her the woes we've had. She tells us some of the sellers have been astoundingly greedy this year. The house of loos, for instance, got its asking price, the seller asked for more, got that, so raised the price again. Now it hasn't sold.

And we already know about the scruples of the Rusty Tractor seller. We curb our optimism.

'You're supposed to be out after twenty minutes,' says the estate agent. 'The seller wants to restrict the length of viewings.'

He does, does he?

She seems to agree that's ridiculous. 'When I told the previous couple, they walked straight out saying they weren't going to be rushed. And you're early so take as long as you want.'

The seller wants to restrict the time people spend here. What doesn't he want them to see? At least we've already scouted its problems, indeed this is our third visit.

We go straight to the trouble spots. The leaks we can cope with. The aircon units, though, are puzzling, not to mention hideous. They're hefty grilles like the end of a van bonnet poking into the room, made of yellowed plastic. They look like they'd choke you with foul vintage smells if you turned them on. In the garden, we find a pair of fans cemented into the wall.

For the aircon units? They are massive, the size of truck wheels, like a cooling installation for a 1980s mainframe computer. Why does the house need this?

We notice the wall under the terrace has a long, deep crack, the kind of thing you see after an earthquake. It probably doesn't matter — or does it?

We still like the house. We make an offer. There's been another, we're told, in the same ballpark. At least it's not the silly money this seller was looking for earlier in the year.

Penny phones about Aardvark. Offer accepted. We did not expect that.

And now we possibly have Rusty Tractor, which is a more manageable price.

We'd better view Aardvark again. Is it really that good?

Calvin returns from holiday. He emails Dave. 'Call me urgently, at 10.30 tomorrow morning.'

That's the time we're viewing Aardvark. What's happened? Why the deadline? Are Mick and Steph finally saying goodbye? We leave a message telling Calvin to call us and we go to Aardvark, trying to guess if we still have buyers.

I still love Aardvark. Dave doesn't.

In the car afterwards, we talk.

'Those oak trees,' says Dave. 'They've grown a lot since the last time. And that's just two months. They're blocking the light into the kitchen. They'll be a constant headache. We'll have to keep pruning them.'

And what's going on under the house with the oak

tree roots and the foundations? No one can answer that.

He's now more attached to Rusty Tractor. He seems more sure of it, even with its infirmities.

I like both of them.

What do we do? Aardvark is ours if we want it.

Rusty Tractor looks more realistic. It has problems, but it was built in the 1930s so it's bedded in and a surveyor can give us proper answers. The Rusty Tractor seller will make a decision about our offer on Monday. Will Mick and Steph wait? If we win the bid, will the seller get greedy and raise the price like last time?

Oh, and Calvin didn't call at 10.30. Even though it was apparently urgent.

When Calvin does call there's no news. It's a routine scolding for not rushing into a deal we're not sure of.

We are so tired of this.

Silly Money

I suppose this was bound to happen.

Mick and Steph want to reduce their offer, says a new email from Calvin.

'They still really want your house, but their costs have risen, the costs of the building work they would like to do.' They would now like to take a whole leg off the price instead of just half.

I fully expect the chimney to chime in with another splutter of mortar.

Calvin has told us before about their building work. It's knocking through a wall and putting a bathroom in the roof. These are matters of choice, not defects that justify a reduction.

Now they're back to the price they started with, funnily enough. We think they never intended to pay more.

We realise something. An arm or a leg make a big difference to us, but not to the estate agent because their commission is roughly the same. They'll hurt if we don't sell at all, but agents on commission are not incentivised to get us the best price.

We should have known this; we've experienced it often enough with literary agents and publishing offers. But that's why Calvin will let our buyers knock so much off.

And it's why Penny lets us keep reducing Aardvark.

This seems like a situation of pots, kettles and name-calling, but the Aardvark sellers aren't fighting back like we are. Now we wonder: is there a reason? Are they keen to be free of that house? Because of the foundations? The shortcuts our surveyor found and maybe others that will come out like guilty secrets? The building guarantee they didn't want to apply for? Is Aardvark actually an albatross?

We have to make a decision and this moment brings clarity. We love Aardvark but we don't trust it.

Mick and Steph have given us a graceful way out. We tell Penny our buyer has cut their offer, which is making everything impossible.

'Oh well,' she says, 'I guess it's not meant to be.' I feel bad because she did a lot of persuading for us. Exit Penny and the Aardvark House.

We're starting to get emails from other estate

agents. They observe that we've sold but not exchanged. Do we realise our house has increased in value? Get a better price with us, they say. One very persistent agent has begun to phone every week. He wants to view the house. Eventually we let him to see what he'll say. He brings a sheaf of brochures for houses he's recently sold. 'I can get you lots of interested buyers,' he says. After he's spent an entire hour pushing his agency to us, he delivers the kicker. 'But it's up to you. You must have the will to sell.'

We know what that means. You mustn't fuss about arms and legs.

Perhaps we should try with a different agent but we don't want to break our agreement with Mick and Steph. That feels like bad behaviour, though behaving well is becoming very hard.

We get a reply about Rusty Tractor. If we could just increase our offer a little.

What would Mick and Steph do about this? They'd make it our problem. We email Calvin. 'Our costs have also changed. We want Mick and Steph to increase their offer.'

This last part is jesting, but only partly.

An instant call from Calvin, who is not jesting at all. He is scandalised. He actually tells us off. 'That's unacceptable. They are building professionals and they know their costs.'

We also know our costs, but apparently it's bad form for us to mention them.

'And if you try to sell your house with another

agent,' says Calvin, 'you'll get even less. Your house has fallen in value.'

Did he know we'd been approached by another agent or was that a lucky guess?

After he rings off we have another moment of clarity. This has gone on too long. We write in an email: 'If Mick and Steph drop the price, by any amount at all, they're out. If this deal works at the price we originally agreed and we get a house we want, we'll proceed. Otherwise you are no longer our agent.'

Calvin calls. The change is immediate. Suddenly he's all lovebombs. 'Mick and Steph really want your house,' he says. 'They've looked at several others and they still love this one.'

Dave says to me afterwards: 'They love the house because they know they're getting a bargain.'

While that's annoying in some ways, we realise it is also a fierce commitment. We aren't as powerless as we think. Maybe.

At first I felt sorry for Mick and Steph. And Calvin. We seemed to be the problem with our bad luck. Now? If everything works out we'll have Rusty Tractor. If not, Mick, Steph and Calvin will be highly annoyed. That seems like a win-win situation.

What am I truly hoping for? Actually, I've no idea.

I Have Fallen Out Of Falling In Love

We hear from the Rusty Tractor agent. We aren't the highest offer, but the highest offer is in a long chain. The seller's circumstances have changed since March. He's been ill. He's split up with his wife and wants to emigrate to Thailand. Honestly, he is serious about moving this time. And our offer is more attractive because we have cash buyers.

We don't fall in love with Rusty Tractor. We loved and lost Aardvark. Hearts are still bruised. Rusty Tractor seems theoretical, like a TV show we are mildly interested in but won't be sad to miss.

After several days of silence, our offer on Rusty Tractor is accepted.

How we have grown up. When our offer on Aardvark was accepted, I went for a run and cocked a snook at the streets I was happy to leave.

Now? I have fallen out of falling in love.

Calvin emails. Mick and Steph are sticking to the deal we originally agreed.

So Rusty Tractor is our house, maybe.

Time to send the surveyor.

'Oh dear,' says the surveyor. 'I recognise that house. I surveyed it for someone in March and had a falling-out with the owner.'

Oh?

'I can't say what I found,' he says. 'Professional confidentiality.'

Still there are a few things he tells us informally. 'There are big aircon units fitted in some of the rooms.'

Yes, the delightful aircon units.

'When you see something weird like that,' says the surveyor, 'you ask yourself why they're there.'

We certainly have been asking that. We also remember the seller wanted to rush buyers through on the open day. So they wouldn't notice.... what?

Dave says: 'I got a general sense from the surveyor that Rusty Tractor has far bigger problems than aircon units.'

I remember the earthquake crack in the wall of the terrace. Though that might be nothing at all.

We email the surveyor. 'If you decide you can

proceed with the survey and it isn't a conflict of interest, let us know. We have already identified concerns with ….'

Surveyor replies. 'On reflection, I never want to deal with that vendor again.'

He must deal with disappointed sellers all the time. Is this one specially monstrous? He might have been if the survey in March found something appalling. Was that why the sale fell through?

Thanks, we reply. 'We have another surveyor we can use, who our solicitor recommended.' We mention his name, for some reason, and the surveyor writes back. 'Haven't heard that name for years. How lovely. He used to be my landlord.'

Do all these people know each other?

How bad is the Rusty Tractor house? We've budgeted for the repairs we've already spotted. Also, to add extra windows because some rooms are gloomy. But we might not be able to afford them if its problems are much more expensive. Do we like the house enough as it is?

'Ready to exchange!' says Calvin.

'We can't let ourselves be bullied into hurrying this,' says Dave.

We call the Rusty Tractor estate agent. 'Can you ask the seller why he fitted the aircon units?'

The estate agent assumes we don't know what aircon is. 'They'll be to keep the roof rooms cool in summer.'

'They're not just in the roof rooms,' we say. 'Look

at the pictures. They're everywhere. Can you ask the seller?'

The estate agent calls later. 'Sorry. I can't get an answer from the seller about the aircon units.'

While Dave is scrutinising the Rusty Tractor sales pictures for the thousandth time, he checks the broadband speed for that road. We assume it's smoking fast, because it's in a neighbourhood where everyone has multiple enormous TVs and home offices.

It's not fast at all. It's the slowest we've seen anywhere.

This is a disaster. I regularly download and upload big book and magazine files. I teach masterclasses via Zoom and VMix and other packages whose names I hear once and never again. I need at least the broadband speed we have in London. The speed at Rusty Tractor is half that. The only solution seems to be to lay a cable ourselves. How expensive is that? And the house is in a private road so getting it organised would be a nightmare.

Enough, I say to Dave. This entire house is a rusty tractor. We don't know how we'd live in it and now we can't work in it.

And joy, Mick and Steph are dropping in again today. We tidy and primp. Drape the throws and scatter the cushions, smile a carefree welcome as they come in.

We go to the car and discuss. How will we confess we're pulling out of the Rusty Tractor house and that's probably the end of everything?

Mick and Steph wave as they leave. Calvin lingers.

'How's it going?'

'A few hiccups,' I say. 'We called a surveyor and he said he surveyed that same house a few months before. He made warning noises.'

As Calvin hears this, he must surely, inside his mind, be clutching his head, sinking into a foetal crouch and performing the Basil Fawlty demented frog dance. His voice and face betray none of this. He replies, with calmness that I have to admire: 'Have you had the survey yet? I don't think you can form a full judgement until you have a survey.'

'We're preparing a backup,' says Dave. I don't know what those backups are but I nod and smile.

Calvin says: 'If you move to a house in the country you'll have a few headaches and you must not be put off.'

'We're not easily put off,' I say. If only he knew the things we've decided not to be put off by.

We go in. We open the windows to expel the slight fragrances they've left, their alien presences. We put the kettle on.

Now, there are emails to write, cancelling the survey of the Rusty Tractor house, removing it from our future, with no idea if another house will come along.

The Stone Tape

A close friend has posted on Facebook that she has a devastating cancer.

She says Facebook is the easiest way to explain to everyone who needs to know. She finishes: 'hug the people you love'.

Comments pour in. A tidal wave of shock, overwhelmingly from those of us who knew her many years before we all entered the digital universe. 'Still hope you'll come here to stay one day,' says one, 'let's make it happen soon.'

Dave and I turn off our computers. We go round the house. Our house, which knows us and her and her partner and so many of the people on that comment thread. The house's cinema of space-time brings them all back. Our dinner parties crowding twelve around a table designed to seat six, where the pudding contained enough alcohol to fuel a plane. Our barbeques where we decreed that the sausage could be regarded as a vegetable.

I grew up in a house that didn't welcome people in. My mother and father kept their friends outside the home, as if they went elsewhere to be themselves. That suited them. It puzzled me. I am fiercely proud of the gatherings this house has seen, and the joy. Our fancy-dress parties where friends from different places met each other and never forgot. 'He was Sideshow Bob with yellow long-johns and a bone through his head.' 'He was the Mexican bandit who was washing up wineglasses in his sombrero and droopy moustache.' 'She was the bearded lady.'

This house is full of deep history, full of us all, our handprints, like the caves of paintings at Lascaux. Dave and I are lazy about redecorating, so the breath of those evenings still hangs somewhere in the molecules of the room.

In 1972 British TV showed *The Stone Tape*, a drama by Nigel Kneale, where an old house keeps memories of events that happened within its walls. The events are sinister, the ghosts are malevolent.

Time is whispering in our walls too. All our excellent times. All our times when we took our continued gatherings for granted.

There have been interruptions. We fall out with one

friend when a book project goes wrong. After a few years Dave meets him in town and brings him back. I hear them unlatch the gate. 'It's like coming home,' says the friend. The estrangement is now a baffling blip, we can't remember why it happened.

Other friends revisit, after much longer absences. They now live far away, some in different continents. They're parents, they're grandparents, they're greyer, but when they come here we are all the same again.

The disappearing past is strong here too. The Mexican bandit, who everyone remembers along with the bearded lady and Sideshow Bob, died shortly after that party in a car crash. This house contains the mystery of entropy and absence.

Our cancer friend and her partner came to one party as Bonnie and Clyde. They are also fixed in the memories that welcome everyone who returns. How can we leave this place? We've been here so long, we have become anchors of time for everyone.

We all gather online now, shocked by this news. We can't change what will happen to Bonnie. But we can all be there, and we're all here now, up and down the years.

Hug the people you love.

*In Which We Save Calvin
From Himself*

'I have a suggestion,' says Calvin. 'What if Mick and Steph contributed to you renting another place?'

They what? They want to pay our rent in another place?

No, we say, we'll carry on as we are. We don't want to get stuck somewhere we don't want to live.

Really, have Mick and Steph offered this? If so, why not give us more for the house in the first place? Last month they were knocking money off.

Has Calvin made this up so that we'll exchange? Because we ended the contract with his agency? He now has to make this sale or it's all been for nothing.

Calvin phones with another idea. 'Why don't you meet Mick and Steph to discuss everything?'

Calvin, you've lost your mind. If we meet them, that will surely be Armageddon.

We reply. 'Here's what will happen if we meet Mick and Steph. We'll tell them, as we've told you, that we never said we would exchange before we had a house to buy, we never intended to rent and we cannot explain how they have this impression.'

Calvin does not continue to suggest we meet them.

Your home, which you have filled with the freight of your years, may have come to you through a fragile web of fabrications that somehow didn't collapse. Or trip over its own shoelaces.

We continue our escapes to the woods. I meet someone in the village post office who I've known for twenty years. When I first met her she was travelling down from London like me, then moved out eight years ago.

Friends say: 'Haven't you moved yet?'

Aardvark would have been ten minutes each way instead of an hour. Rusty Tractor would have been twenty. And much less petrol because there would be no stop-start London traffic.

'If this falls through,' says Dave, 'and we lose our buyers, I'm going to take you on holiday to a tower.'

Wait. Here's a good house on Rightmove. It's 1970s, updated with glass and bright, bold spaces. We book a viewing. On the day, the estate agent cancels. The owners have tested positive for Covid.

Even microbes want to spoil our plans, so we go on holiday to a tower.

We come back. And Mick and Steph are still with us. It is still going on.

Turn Right At The Rainbow

'Turn right at the rainbow,' says Dave, with a surprised lift in his voice as he realises how that sounds.

He is reading directions off my phone.

The rainbow is the Rainbow; a pub, not a weather phenomenon, but those words send us into a flight of nonsense.

'Turn right at the rainbow,' we muse, because, as writers, we're always sweating for a good line and it never arrives when we need it. Then, while we're doing something else, along comes a piece of accidental poetry, brazen as anything.

Today, though, we need significant words. We've had an unusual afternoon.

Turn Right At The Rainbow

For once we're not househunting. We've been visiting Bonnie and Clyde, Bonnie who has the cancer diagnosis. She has had gruelling treatments. We feared we might find her frail and changed, but she was exactly her old self. We sat in their garden roaring with laughter as always, talking about usual things like friends and films and holidays, and unusual things like bucket lists.

Now we drive away, full of affection, relief, gratitude and hope, and Dave, reading the directions on my phone, says 'Turn right at the rainbow.'

Suddenly we're in a musical, about to sing the big number about our whole situation. Our mistravels as we dabble with numerous possible destinies, believing in each one until it falls down. Now this afternoon, complicated and remarkable, is a complete recalibration of everyone's ideas about luck and odds, and what we do with the cards that fate deals to us.

Turn right at the rainbow; that's all we can hope to do. We decide it's funny too, because, as poetry, it's pretty terrible.

Happenstance

I am keen on a lot more houses than Dave is. This is a problem.

There's a house I feel a sense of kinship with. Ten years ago I saw it being born. As I passed it day by day I watched a bungalow turn to dust and a handsome white townhouse rise in its place. I coveted it in my usual wishful-thinking way, and now, just as we need a house, it's for sale. Destiny?

After the viewing there's a brittle atmosphere in the car.

'That garden slopes up at the back,' says Dave. 'The ground floor will always be dark.'

I remind him of its virtues. Light from above in two rooms. Stylish proportions and feel. Solid build quality. Tiny garden. I'm sold.

'It's got too many bathrooms.'

'Bathrooms don't harm anyone.'

But Dave doesn't like the house, and that can't be argued away. This is not The One.

But hurrah, here is one we both like. It's a period house that has had its middle demolished to divide it in two. The estate agent sends me a picture of the original master bathroom, which was in one of the demolished areas. It is hauntingly beautiful, lined with golden mosaic tiles like the set for a Hollywood epic about King Midas, an opulent ghost clinging between the two houses where there is now a hedge and a side alleyway. Like Great Down, it feels rich with stories. I want to live there and bring our people.

When we view it the downstairs is dark because the house is surrounded by chestnut trees. But they're just trees. We can cut them down. This is The One.

No we can't cut the trees down. Each tree — every one of them — has a preservation order and we can't touch them. The house is condemned to perpetual gloom. This is not The One.

Both houses remain unsold week after week as we continue to search. I ask myself. Could they become an eighty instead of a fifty? We could say the word and start to make them ours.

Calvin's getting antsy. Every day there's a telling-off.

'It's his attitude that really annoys me,' says Dave. 'He always seems to be saying "must try harder". Have we thought of looking at cheaper places? Cheaper locations? Have we realised we might lose our buyers?

Dave replies to Calvin, gently and firmly. 'Losing our buyers would be awful. But, and we know we've said this before, it would be more awful to swap a house we like for a house we don't.'

Dave has been playing with an AI art program. We tell it to draw 'a telling-off from Calvin'. It doesn't know what a telling-off is, or a Calvin, and gives us a misty multicoloured blob with Halloween eye-holes.

We try to appease Calvin with numbers, like we did with Alvin. We're investigating four houses this week. Three next week. They don't turn into viewings but Calvin seems quieted. Calvin leaves messages on Dave's mobile, then complains we haven't replied, but we've told him Dave can never retrieve them because the voicemail works in mysterious ways. Use our email and landline if you want to contact us, we tell him, but he continues to talk to the voicemail.

Really we are all marking time until something new happens; Dave and I are reporting meaningless numbers, Calvin is leaving messages he knows we'll never find.

One morning Calvin says: 'Your buyers have found another house but they like yours more. If you exchange by the end of the week with a long completion date... Think about it.'

So that's it.

I do a weights class, clattering the barbell crossly. I thought I would accept this moment when it came, but I feel I've had to give up. I hate that. It must be somebody's fault. Mick and Steph's; they made a mean offer that simply wasn't enough. If we'd known we would have told Calvin to keep looking for other buyers. It's Calvin's fault too. He should have pushed back at them instead of telling us we were the problem. Though actually, he's acting for the deal, and that's his real job.

There are bigger reasons, which are beyond the struggles of a few people who are trying to find a house or make a living. A war in Ukraine. Inflation. Brexit and the pandemic lockdown. A government that has no idea what to do. That's where blame belongs, on the bummest of bum years for the entire world.

When I check my emails, estate agents are still sending us houses, full of optimism. Looking at them is like drowning in sameness. But I spot a possibility.

It's a good-looking new-build I saw for sale a few months ago. I called the estate agent about it but they never replied. Now here it is again. We are not defeated. I call the agent.

The house has just had an offer. It has been on Rightmove for mere minutes. How does anyone do this?

I shouldn't be thinking about houses right now. I am giving a talk at a festival this evening about a couple of my books. I've been looking forward to it, but this non-moving move is eating my brain.

The next morning, a glimmer of hope. That house

is back on the market. So soon? What happened?

Never mind that. I show it to Dave. 'Let's see this one. Tomorrow.'

'We can't see it tomorrow. It'll have to be Friday.'

I give him my sternest look.

Okay, he says.

We get the viewing.

This is a last ditch. My chance to not give up.

The builders are still finishing and the sales pictures are computer generated, but we can tell the house has the space and light we need. Its garden is pleasingly small. It's built in an orchard that originally belonged to the house next door. As we walk around, we know how we'll use each room. We make an offer there and then. The only other time we've done that is with Aardvark.

The estate agent says, in a severe tone: 'Other people are viewing the house'. We've seen that reaction before. Estate agents hate it if you offer before you've been asked. They should be doing their happy dance. Instead they look perplexed and annoyed, like cats in YouTube videos.

As we leave, another car is pulling in. A Porsche.

Fat chance we can outbid the owners of a Porsche.

We drive home, not daring to speak. This could be the house. If the Porsche people don't also bid. If Mick and Steph haven't bailed. We've grabbed this house as fast as anyone can, but it might be too late.

The estate agent calls. Our offer is accepted if we pay a token deposit immediately.

We call Calvin. He's already had a call to check us out. He's trying to contact Mick and Steph but they aren't answering.

Perhaps it's over. What a shame.

The more we think about this house, the more it feels right. It even has a room in the roof, like we have in London. We can work in the rooms on the middle floor and sleep at the top.

Finding it is happenstance, but we know one happenstance isn't enough. We need several more, and all at the right time.

'Moving house, if you buy and sell in one chain, you need to win two lotteries at the same time,' says a friend. Only two? I'd say that's an underestimate.

The weekend passes. Monday passes. Tuesday. What does this silence mean? If Mick and Steph have exchanged on something else, we'll surely be put out of our misery. Or will we? Calvin must think we deserve a dose of misery.

Wednesday, a call from the estate agent of the house we've offered on. Everything's hunky dory. She's talked to Calvin.

We didn't know about that.

After phenomenal pestering, Dave gets Calvin's office on the phone, but not Calvin himself. We get Alvin.

'There are three conditions,' says Alvin. 'First, you must exchange in four weeks.'

I can see why Calvin isn't delivering this in person.

We explain. 'We can't exchange in four weeks. The

builders are still in the house and won't finish for at least six.'

'But you can exchange,' says Alvin.

'If we do that, the builder has no incentive to finish.'

Alvin moves to point two. 'Mick and Steph want to complete in January.'

January is three months away. We can't just pick a completion date out of a hat. We tell him we'll agree a date that's reasonable for all, including us.

'And point three,' says Alvin. 'Mick and Steph want to drop the price, as discussed before. House prices have fallen.'

Sigh. Have they not learned?

In that case, we say, we're putting it back on the market.

And Mick and Steph can sulk in their rental, counting the cost of skinflinting.

Afterwards, we open wine.

'Mick and Steph do this whenever we make an offer. They hope we'll be desperate and they can pull the rug away.'

'I've looked them up,' says Dave. 'They used to be management consultants.'

This seems incredibly funny. 'Do they think they are skilled negotiators?'

'I think we can see their style of negotiation.'

'Tough titty. It's either their house or it's ours, and at the moment it's ours.'

This is how we end up where we are. It's not just timing or the luck of the market. It's the people we are and the people we're dealing with, and how we all get along. Or don't.

But unexpectedly, Alvin calls back. It seems we're going ahead.

So here I'll introduce another person: Vera, the estate agent for the house in the orchard. The Windfall House.

It's Happening

The Chain Is Humming

The Windfall House is proceeding. We have been back to measure cupboards, take pictures of electric sockets and window positions. We have chosen the paint colour for the dining room, matched to the dining room of our own house, a duck-egg blue from an oriental fan that hangs on the wall.

Bit by bit, Windfall is claiming us, though we are being cautious in case Mick and Steph decide to prove what hardass negotiators they are.

One of my college friends is also moving. Sarah has a house by a Scottish loch. It's beautiful but remote, so she and

The Chain Is Humming

her husband decide to move back to civilisation. Soon they have a buyer and are exchanging on another dream house, in a bay with a lighthouse and a view of the sea.

In a mere few months they have won the two necessary lotteries, while we have taken all year.

Sarah shares pictures of the final days. The rooms of the old house full and lived in, then emptied. It looks forlorn but she says she's so busy it doesn't make much impression. There are many people to say goodbye to. A Scottish loch community is so different from London, when you can spend thirty years in a street and not know any of your neighbours.

Sarah is an artist. Some of these local friends came to her through art life. They are other artists, picture framers, local couriers. Art is out for all to see. Writing is not. No one can watch our creations take shape. Once finished, the book operates as a private event inside the reader's imagination, not observable by onlookers. When we work with other creative people that is also invisible, in the worldwide mind of the internet. Every house on our street might be home to a busy author and nobody would know. But art makes friends. When Sarah visits her new village she spots an exhibition and is soon swapping numbers with the artists there for when she'll arrive properly.

Sarah updates her photo diary; last packing, last lattes, last book club meeting, last Scrabble game, last sunset over the loch, last load leaving in the lorry.

By tomorrow, new people will be arriving here, and

they are currently on their own list of lasts, as are the people in Sarah's new home by the lighthouse. The chain is humming, the end of one journey will join the start of another and complete the circuit of fates. It's happening for all these people on this particular upcoming date, like Christmas.

As I write wishing her luck, she sends another message. A vital document has been delayed by postal strikes. They thought they were thoroughly prepared. Now there are frantic calls and exasperating silences. Eventually a solution is found. Moving day should have started with a leisurely mooch to the new place, appreciating each unique unfolding moment. Instead it's a 6am dash up the motorway to a far city, carrying the weight of the whole chain, where the solicitor is waiting with another copy.

They sign the document. Then all the vehicles and people set out and the celestial machine is in motion.

Just in case you thought it should be easy.

Gone But Not Forgotten

I'm catching up with another college friend. Meeting is a major expedition across two counties.

'Let's find somewhere half-way between London and Chelmsford.'

'LOL. We moved from Chelmsford about ten years ago.'

'But we've been sending your Christmas cards there. And our thrilling Christmas letter.'

'They're going to feel a bit left out this year.'

Mick and Steph, you might remove our paint colours, our curtains, our kitchen, our carpets, our walls and windows, but you'll find it harder to remove us. Numerous systems, many we cannot reach, will still attach this house to us. In those systems we will always be here, and you are the surprise.

The Windfall House is different. It stands on virgin soil. On Google Earth the plot is a garden with two sheds. No one has had a house here before. We will be its first.

We Are Its First

Our solicitor emails. 'I have completed my report as far as I am able. Do you want this now in the knowledge that the seller still has crucial documents to deliver? The contract and other documents could follow once we are confident that all is in order. I have chased your seller's estate agent.'

The seller's estate agent is Vera. We chase her too. She tells us off.

'I thought you wanted to move as quickly as possible,' she says. 'Why is your solicitor delaying?'

Vera has received the same blame training as Calvin.

The documents arrive. A slab of 300 A4

pages. Yes, I look at them, because this is the story of the land that's about to become our house. There are proposed plans, modifications, endless permissions, searches, certificates. Dave and I once dreamed of building our own house if we could find a plot of land. Perhaps it's a good thing we didn't because this paperchase looks gruelling.

Some of the investigations are arcane and weird. One is 'chancel repair'. Our solicitor has helpfully explained. 'Certain properties could be obliged to pay towards the cost of repairing the chancel of the parish church even if the church is some distance from the house. The liability might be substantial.' She gives an example. In Warwickshire in 2003, the council tried to argue the residents should pay £186,000 for church repairs.

The chancel, she adds, because these documents like to be wordy, is the part of a church near the altar, reserved for the clergy and choir. So although you might be obliged to fund it, you wouldn't be allowed in there yourself. God moves in mysterious ways and some of them are known only to lawyers.

The Windfall House, says our legal document, has no recorded potential for chancel repair liability.

Another who-would-have-thought-it document is an insurance policy to confirm that all previous sales of the site were lawful. There are dates from 1899, then 1900, then 1907. So 1899 is the first time this ground was claimed from the wild. The document gives names, a list like a dynasty in a historical novel. Henry Van

Den Bergh sold it in 1899 to Alfred Augustus Gale. Alfred Augustus Gale sold it in 1900 to Mary Ann Jauncey and The Honourable Cecil Josephine Sandys, an interesting mix of genders there. Henry Van Den Berg still had an interest because he sold another piece of it in 1907 to William Shears. If you are buying a house, did you know this is in your paperwork? A list of the property's significant people, stitched into documents that no one will read unless they're a lawyer. Or a writer. Or anyone who has spent a long, long time getting to this moment.

A cynic would say it's evidence of how ingenious the insurance industry is, dreaming up products for obscure and unlikely risks, and also of the many ways solicitors can find to spend our money, but the result is this family tree for the house, a family tree of people I could research to discover what they did on this patch of land that will soon be ours, where they came from and where they went afterwards. From Henry Van Den Bergh all the way to Charles Henrikson, who sold it to the builder of the Windfall House in 2022.

And when this document is compiled again, another line will be added. Roz and Dave Morris.

Auld Acquaintance

With no need to check Rightmove any more, I am free for other kinds of online timewasting. One evening I look for the other places I've lived in.

The flat in south-east London, where I lived before I met Dave. I discover it has never been on the market since I left. My ex-partner must still own it.

The home before that, though, the flat in West Hampstead from Beginning A London Life, has recently been sold. With a fluke of timing, it came on the market as we started looking earlier this year. Not that it would have suited me and Dave, but it is a considerable coincidence. I don't have many former addresses, and one of them is about to be sold.

A person who believed in spooky connectedness would take it to heart. I'm thinking here of my father with his tireless search for comforting alignments (remember him adding up the digits in phone numbers). This coincidence I've discovered of the sale of the West Hampstead flat would be a heavenly sign, for him, that Dave and I are on the threshold of a big change and that it will really happen. Right now, I'm inclined to agree.

I poke through the estate agent pictures of the West Hampstead flat. It is so nice that the internet has made this possible. I compare my memories of the lived-in place to the online pictures with their sales gloss. What do I recognise? Not much. Some of the rooms I never went in because they belonged to other tenants and we hardly saw each other. We lived different routines. We used the kitchen at different times, came and went at different times.

I have a fresh thought that entertains me. They are as human as I am, and surely as prone to nostalgia. At some point recently they might have discovered, like I have this evening, that the place has sold. And in a way it's like the old days, when we glanced off each other in roughly the same part of space-time, and nodded hello.

The Snagging Survey

Vera has, for the past two weeks, been calling every day to say 'Why is your solicitor delaying?'

Our solicitor says: 'I'm waiting for your seller to send me documents.'

'I'll chase,' says Vera.

Then: 'They've now supplied all the documents.'

'No they haven't,' says our solicitor. She adds: 'I know estate agents would like us to move faster but it has to be done properly and that is that.'

Vera emails. 'I want to suggest a moving date of Friday 13th January.'

That sounds like a terrible idea, and

not just because it's Friday the 13th. Today's date is 13th December. We haven't been able to book a survey. The builders are still in the Windfall House and they'll soon stop for Christmas.

Also, we haven't begun to pack because moving still seems so unlikely, in spite of everything. That worries me, but it doesn't seem to worry Dave.

Anyway, where did Vera get this date of 13th January? Did she cast the runes?

'We'll set a moving date after the survey results,' we say.

'Ah, you don't need a survey,' says Vera. 'It's a new house. Save your money.'

Aardvark was a new house. The survey was most enlightening.

A day later, Vera calls. 'Windfall is ready for its survey! It should be straightforward. Just a snagging check.'

The surveyor goes to the Windfall House and sends his report. It is not straightforward.

Aardvark had perhaps twenty problems. Windfall has hundreds.

Some are minor: light switches not connected, unfinished plumbing and radiators with no flow. Some are horrors: several of the windows have bowed and at least two have spontaneously cracked. The front door has warped and doesn't fit. Why wasn't this noticed by the builders?

Anyway, that means replacing them all.

One window, in the downstairs loo, has been

installed on the wonk. The surveyor's pic shows it against a spirit level. This will drive us nuts because we'll always know. And the surveyor says it might be a sign that the building has major settlement problems, which might be why so many other windows have bowed and broken. And if so, the replacements will break all over again.

There is also a lot of incomplete pointing and rendering in the gutters, and the floor in the top bathroom isn't strong enough for the weight of the shower. It needs another joist, which means ripping everything up, or the shower seal will crack and leak into the room below. The best horror of all is an air brick placed at ground level in one of the walls, so the foundations will flood after just an inch of rainfall. Permanent damp under the house.

We are shocked. We thought the biggest snag would be Mick and Steph's great price gunfight on exchange day. We didn't dream the biggest snag would be an unfinished and shoddy house.

We tell Vera. She writes back, beginning, somehow, by blaming us.

'I'm sorry this was the case. As you are aware the survey and solicitors are being rushed as we have been told it's mandatory for your buyer that the chain exchanges this side of Christmas. On this basis what do you want to do? We can exchange before Christmas and complete the snagging between exchange and completion. This can be written into the contracts. Or we can delay exchange and inform your buyer. As an

The Snagging Survey

additional thought, would you appreciate a visit to the house with the seller to maybe ease some concerns?'

We're glad she mentioned the seller. We ask her to take the problems to him and bring us his answers.

Vera says: 'yes of course, I'll do that'. No, that's what she doesn't do. She says: 'When I spoke to the surveyor, he advised that the seller only needed to tie up loose ends and it wasn't a large amount of work.'

She's telling us the surveyor didn't say what he said.

She doesn't want to talk to the seller about this. Why not?

So we tell her again and she says. 'Maybe your surveyor can provide clarification?'

As a tactic it's fascinating: if the facts don't suit her, pretend she isn't being told them.

Perhaps a different angle will get answers. We ask about the building guarantees and sign-offs for the Windfall House. What did the inspectors say about these issues?

Short answer: it does not have its guarantees.

The Vera answer is elaborate and involves a blizzard of dates. 'The seller says the final visit for building regulations is 21st December, then the warranty provider will issue the certificates, probably in the first week of January, which is why the seller suggested 13th January for completion, knowing that would give him enough time to have everything done.'

These dates are probably supposed to make us feel that everything is under control, but any fool can see the house can't be fixed by 13th January. It won't be fit to live in. They have to rip up the top floor to add a joist to support the bathroom. Dig out the misplaced airbrick and bash another hole to re-site it. Replace windows and doors, which won't be delivered for months.

As for the guarantees and warranties, will the seller's next move be a request to forget about them, like Aardvark?

Dave emails our solicitor. 'Vera says these snagging issues can be written into the contract, but is it advisable to exchange with them outstanding? How would we set a completion date if we don't know when the seller will have the house ready? Is this routine with new builds? How can we be certain the seller will fix the problems once we've exchanged?'

Our solicitor replies. 'I have told the other side there are these issues. Some of the points raised by the surveyor I would not call "snagging" so we need to carefully consider the timeframe. I will make sure you are protected. Vera is trying to help but there are legal implications that the seller's solicitor has to bear in mind if the property is not ready by the fixed completion date.'

You might be wondering about Calvin. Here he is.

'Your house is the oldest sale in our pipeline by over four months. Since it has been under offer, we have exchanged on 276 properties. Why are you delaying so much? I know many people who've bought a house that was no more than a hole in the ground.'

Goody for them. We would not do that.

Calvin emails again. 'If we haven't exchanged before Christmas, none of this will matter because you will not have a buyer. To be frank, it is miraculous that they are still there.' He sends a link. 'Here is a house your buyers are viewing today, just up the road from you, same style, for two legs less.'

Vera calls. She's the very embodiment of innocence. 'I thought your priority was to exchange ASAP. You'll lose your buyers. And if you lose your buyers, the seller will put the house back on the market.'

So we tell Vera: 'Ask the seller to answer our questions. We've identified serious faults with the house and the seller hasn't made any response. There were other buyers before us, weren't there, who pulled out. Why is that? Do you not think we should find a solution?'

Vera says: 'Are you trying to call your buyers' bluff?'

So it goes, on and on. Vera loops through her blame repertoire a few more times, telling us we haven't given her the report. Or she wields her dates: 'Everything will be sorted out by 10th January.'

We keep stating the obvious. 'What does the seller say? In all your emails, there has not been an answer from him.' Is no one is hearing this?

No, they are hearing this. They are telling us they don't have to fix the problems because there is no time.

Everyone is furious. We are furious with the seller for being evasive and dishonest. We are furious with Vera, who is obfuscating and obstructing, quite brazenly, in the hope we'll give in and exchange.

I always thought this might end with our buyers pulling a nasty trick on exchange day. I didn't think it would end like this, in an impossible impasse. What a huge waste of stress and money.

Christmas cards are arriving. One says: 'You are the only people in our forty-year-old address book who have never changed their address.'

Friends arrive for the Christmas gaming special. In the days before the Covid lockdown, this used to be a regular event. We also held a spring special, a summer special, an autumn special. Before that there were fortnightlies, when everyone lived close enough to travel by Tube or bike, and on one occasion helped us chase away burglars and restore the house to good spirits. Over the years, the seasonal specials became cherished reunions of the old gang, until Covid.

This is the first gaming special since the pandemic. People arrive from Oxford. From Bristol. From Essex. From high up in Buckinghamshire, which will have been a drive of four hours. For some of us, it's the first time we've met in person, with handshakes and hugs, for three years.

'This might be the last game here,' says more than one person, sure that we are moving at last, and then we tell our tale. Complicated expressions cross faces. If the game we were playing was poker, they would all be terrible at it. They are sorry we've had such trouble but cannot hide their delight.

What Vera and Calvin Did Next

New year arrives. We can't trust the seller of the Windfall House so we're not going to buy it. We paid him a deposit. How to get it back? Presumably if we pull out, we don't get refunded.

But he needs to sell, so we'll wait until he backs out.

Meanwhile, should we keep looking? We still have an offer for our house, which we might as well take out for exercise. Though that seems very theoretical now.

We look at a house that's been on our radar for a while. New. Full of light, by a builder with a solid reputation. But it's a bit too far to drive, nearly an hour from where we want to be. Why are we viewing it?

The hunting instinct never dies, even if the pursuit seems futile.

Vera phones. 'Happy new year. I have news. The seller of the Windfall House has gone back to a previous offer, which is higher, and they've nearly done the conveyancing and don't mind the problems you found in the survey.'

This is confusing, so I'll spell it out. We've been gazumped.

That's unexpected.

But it gets us nicely off the hook.

I'm listening on the other extension as Dave replies. 'Good, he can give us our deposit back.'

Vera goes silent, then repeats. 'I said, the seller has gone back to the previous buyer, who has now reinstated their offer.'

'Good. Now, our deposit.'

A stumbling kind of silence as Vera computes. Clearly she didn't expect this reply. She says: 'You see, he couldn't fix the points you mentioned by 10th January. You may not realise how long they would take.'

This conversation is becoming very strange.

Dave says: 'We do realise. That's why we asked to talk about them properly. But you kept saying they'd be fixed by 10th January.'

'And now,' says Vera, as if Dave has said nothing at all, 'the previous buyer has come back with their offer. Which is higher.'

'Yes, you said,' replies Dave. 'So the seller will be taking that offer and can give us our deposit back.'

Vera says: 'Do you want to think about that and get back to me?' She hangs up.

'What is going on?' says Dave to me. 'I thought we were finished.'

Then Calvin emails. 'Happy new year. I have had a call from Vera. I understand that because of the line you were taking prior to the break, the seller has decided to switch to the previous buyer. My understanding is that they have reinstated their offer, which is higher than yours, and have guaranteed exchanging prior to the end of the month, and have inspected the property and don't believe it needs the significant works you've requested. I haven't seen the house so I can't comment directly, but it does seem odd that someone is willing to gazump your offer and exchange in under a month if the work is as necessary as previously stated. '

Calvin, it's more than odd.

'From conversations with Vera,' says Calvin, 'I can see a path to getting this done.'

It's all nonsense. If they really had a better offer, they'd ditch us and take it.

It's over. We need to get on with our lives. And so do Mick and Steph.

But it isn't over for Calvin and Vera. They are frantic to make us exchange.

For so long we have felt powerless, trying to get straight answers from Calvin and Vera. Now we don't care, but Calvin and Vera care a great deal. Let's sit back and enjoy the show.

Did they think this ploy with a returning buyer would work? If so, they could have made it plausible. They could have said the other buyer had made a matching offer. Instead they've overplayed their hand, perhaps to make us panic that we might have to pay more if we don't shut up and sign. And they've hoist themselves with their own canard.

Or maybe Vera got the plan wrong. Perhaps she was supposed to say there was another offer, but decided to embellish. 'The original buyers are back, and they offered a lot more and they'll exchange immediately.' Because she seemed surprised when we said, 'Well the seller will take their offer, won't he?'

Now Calvin's trying to stick it back together by saying it's our fault because we made a fuss about the survey, and that if we drop that the seller will ignore the much better offer. What?

'As a study in game theory, it's hilarious,' says Dave, who has designed numerous games over the years.

What's Calvin saying to Vera now? Oh for a hidden camera.

Calvin calls again. He's not leaving us alone. 'You need to make a decision on whether you want to move or not. Often in property transactions, one has to take the broader view. I am not sure what the value of works you would want to do at this house are, but I suggest you pit this against the fact that you will be looking at a much-reduced sale price on your house if we were to sell it again.'

It's the 'will-to-sell' pep-talk from the estate agent's standard playbook. His job is simply to get us out, it doesn't matter where to. A leaky building site with broken windows or, as he said himself, a hole in the ground. That's not his concern and, after all, he hasn't taken a Hippocratic oath to do no harm. Also, I think he's forgotten we ended the agency agreement and he won't be selling the house for us again.

Still, he needs a reply.

We pretend we believe their ridiculous story.

'Yes, we just spoke to Vera. The original buyer has come back at an offer considerably above ours. Clearly we can't now negotiate about the defects. We will look for another house.'

We're not looking for another house but we hope he understands the message. We're done with Windfall.

Vera is also waiting for an answer.

'We will not be raising our offer. We understand the seller will go with the other offer. Therefore he will return our £1000 securing deposit. Our bank details are etc.'

This is the end. This email says so.

No, it's not the end.

Vera leaves a phone message. Please call.

'She needs to grovel,' I say. 'There is no other buyer and she's in deep do-do.'

'Let's ignore her. We've got things to do.'

The phone rings.

'Ah hello Vera,' says Dave. Then he says: 'I had a feeling they might do that,' and I hear a twitch of a smile in his voice. He adds: 'We've told our solicitor to stop everything. We were told we were gazumped.'

There is a torrent of babble. It sounds squeaky and hysterical.

Dave is grinning when he puts the phone down. 'The other buyer has withdrawn, she says. They were upset because it's so competitive.'

That's very, very funny.

'Vera said: "I suspect they got carried away with the excitement of getting the house again and didn't think".'

'Certainly someone got carried away.'

'Vera said: "We don't like getting this reputation, so we're coming back with our tail between our legs".'

'And what about the survey?'

'She says we might have to compromise and accept there might be building work after we move in. But we could complete in six weeks.'

Might. Could. Here's another thing to know about Vera. She does all her promising on the phone, never in writing.

In case you're wondering, we are not tempted.

We spell it out. The answer is No. We do not have any faith in how negotiations will be handled. The seller could have talked honestly about the problems and Mick and Steph would have known an exchange was coming if they felt like waiting. Instead Vera told us we'd been gazumped. So: No. And we don't expect

Mick and Steph to hang around, nor do we blame them. Have we said enough Nos?

It seems we have not. Calvin mounts a fresh attack. Mick and Steph have made an offer on a nearby house. He sends us the brochure to try and stir us up, as though he's never sent it before. Actually this is the third time.

'If we can exchange right now I think I can persuade Mick and Steph. Otherwise they will proceed with this other house.'

Proceed they must, we say.

As the carrot hasn't worked, Calvin charges in with the stick. 'If you lose your buyer, and your house is marketed again, it will be at a much-reduced figure. You'll start the whole process again which as we know isn't always smooth sailing. Your house was on for six months-'

For the record, it was four-and-a-half months.

'... on for six months in the best market of the last decade and now it would be at least a leg less, maybe more. And your chance of finding a chain-free or cash buyer is slim. I know what I would do.'

Here he has said something that deserves serious consideration. He knows what he would do, or what he wishes we would do, but it's not what we would actually do. He has never listened to this, even though we've told him almost daily. We're not looking for just a move or a sale. We're looking for a home we can be sure of.

Like the one we would be leaving.

That's enough. We confirm to our solicitor. Stop everything.

She writes back. 'The seller has come back to say they are still happy to sell to you! Therefore, I am double-checking that you are no longer interested in continuing with this contract.'

Are we in a panto? We say 'oh no we're not'. They say 'oh yes you are'.

A call from Calvin's office. Not Calvin. He is probably beyond civilised speech now. It's Alvin. Are we sure? Mick and Steph would still rather have our house. They like it sooooo much. They've hung on so long.

No, we say. That's it. 'We're sorry it's worked out like this' says Dave to Alvin. 'If Mick and Steph run into us in the street, I wouldn't blame them if they cut us dead.'

A shocked noise, then: 'I know they were frustrated but I don't think you have to fear they'd resort to violence...'

Alvin took the figure of speech literally.

We're laughing, but we're also licking our wounds. We made substantial commitments, which we can measure in fees paid to solicitors and surveyors. And tanks of petrol. And so many months of stress and hope.

We ask Vera for our deposit back. No, she says. The seller is allowed to deduct reasonable expenses. What expenses? We were told we could choose the dining room paint colour but apparently it's not acceptable for general selling. It has to be redone, which, plus labour, amounts to our deposit. That's simply spiteful and also against the spirit of the deposit, which was supposed to secure us against gazumping. But we can't pursue it without legal guns and we've already spent too much with nothing to show. And we certainly can't expect Vera to argue for us.

We notice the solicitor doesn't encourage us to pursue the deposit.

The seller has a development company so I write a blistering review on Trustpilot that will be found if anyone researches them in future.

For the first time in many months, there are no more communications from Calvin. Calvin is gone.

Vera isn't. We're still on her agency's list as potential buyers. They continue to send properties. Soon they send the very house we have just run away from. Now the brochure has real interior photos instead of computer-imagined ones. I note the dining room has the paint colour we chose.

A few months later, our solicitor writes. A lawyer who is now processing the Windfall House has forgotten to order searches, the documents in which, on an innocent and hopeful afternoon, I enjoyed discovering the names of the previous people in the house's history. Now there's big trouble because the searches have been forgotten. Our solicitor has been asked if we'll sell them ours. 'How much was the deposit?!' she says.

We laugh. We remind her.

It's Happening

'Ah, I was being a bit facetious,' she says. 'I would imagine they are thinking of a nominal amount of £50. Or you could say you are disinclined to offer the search.'

Although this is frustrating for the new buyer, it's much worse for Vera and the Windfall House seller. Let them suffer the delay, pay full price for a fast-tracked search and wait a bit longer.

Knowing how this will vex Vera, who cannot abide delays, or disobedience from a buyer or solicitor, we allow ourselves one of those smiles.

The Dust Is Settling

As I edit this book a year on, I need to check a detail of the first house we made a bid on. The one whose seller backed out, even though we met his asking price. If that had gone differently, this adventure would have been mighty short. Did they ever move?

They didn't. The house never sold.

Rusty Tractor also came up in the search. It was in the same road. It never got another buyer. It isn't currently up for sale.

There was a third house we nearly saw in that road. When we lost the first one, the estate agent promised us a sneak preview. They were preparing the brochure to launch it the next week. It never came to market at all.

I think of the estate agents for those houses. All the hours they spent talking to sellers, preparing sales documents, gathering buyers for viewings and open days. Then chasing offers, trying to get buyers and sellers to agree, keeping the peace in the chain. All came to nothing. A year on, the people who were trying to sell those houses are still there.

This is just three houses, in one short cul-de-sac. Is this typical?

I begin to understand why estate agents are so desperate to railroad a sale no matter what. We think they can't behave decently and honestly. They must think buyers and sellers are spoilt children who need to wake up to the real world. Any estate agents who are reading, you'll be reporting us for mental cruelty.

And what about the people who were selling? When we viewed a house I'd always ask why they wanted to move. I wanted evidence of strong motivation, and everyone seemed convincing. Family reasons, health reasons, seeking a new start in a different place. We heard, many times, that the sellers would rent if their buyer required a quick move. Would they really or did the estate agents just say that, hoping to sort it out later? Remember the renting discussions with Calvin.

But Dave and I put our faith in the sellers' stories, because we wanted to believe. And when you know what's in their cupboards, you think you know what's in their hearts.

The Dust Is Settling

The three houses in that one road. Those were three stories that didn't happen. The first was for sale because the seller was ready to downsize. They didn't downsize. Rusty Tractor came to us twice. The first time, the seller raised his price, got an offer, then lost it. When he came back we were told he meant it this time. He'd been ill. His marriage was breaking up. He was going to move to Thailand, and I believed that because he had life-size Buddha statues in the lounge, though they might have been bought at John Lewis. Now, a year later, the house hasn't sold and he's still waiting for the life change.

I begin an odyssey through other houses that were possibles. How many of these sellers began new chapters?

The house with all the loos and the dismal prisoner annexe, whose owners were also downsizing, and small wonder. This is the house we were told had sold for a greedy whack above asking price. It didn't. Today it's still on the market, sold subject to contract but for much less. Three entire legs less, which must be painful, especially after the price 'madness' so gleefully celebrated by the estate agent.

The Waltons house with the cult assembly rooms that gave me strange dreams, where the estate agent found a credit card that bore our names, as if we were being placed there by a godlike scriptwriter. It did sell. Those people are onto their new lives.

The Chandeliers House sold. So did the bungalow with the groovy layout, where we imagined ourselves boldly removing walls, with no idea whether that would correct its wrongness. So did the house owned by the hundred-year-old lady, which Dave had a fifty-year nodding acquaintance with. The Windfall House sold, God help the new owners.

The house converted from a 1920s mansion, with the chilly half-ballroom between the hall and kitchen? It never sold. Its people are still rattling in there.

Great Down sold, to my regret. I remember its sellers were moving to Devon. It seems they really did.

The Aardvark House hasn't sold. And now I'd better stop looking.

A few bits of footnotery.

I must thank the friends who have helped this story along in numerous ways, particularly Peter Snell, David Bodanis, and, of course, Dave Morris. Also Leo Hartas for the cover.

I must tell you about the friend I mentioned in Where You Belong, who writes historical and alternate history novels inspired by his home town in the Surrey Hills. His name is John Whitbourn. All his work is worth a look, but for starters try his series of short stories, *The Binscombe Tales*, a collection of eerie *Twilight-Zone* happenings, with characters and mysteries as ancient as the land. You'll never talk to a stranger at a bus stop again.

While we're talking about mysteries in the land, you might enjoy watching Alan Garner talking about the woods and mines in the Weirdstoned pieces. YouTube has the documentary I mentioned in Thin

Places. It's called *The Edge of the Ceiling* and it's made by Granada Television, broadcast in June 1980. My friend on the grey horse is at 13.28. (Quick aside: Thin Places is included in a collection of essays to be published by Manchester University Press in 2026, *Alan Garner And The Work of Time*.)

You might also like the documentary from 1973 about Alan Garner's novel *Red Shift*. He visits his former home in Alderley Edge, where his family had lived for 300 years, and gets a nasty surprise. The house is being dismantled and rebuilt. He delivers a shocked piece to camera, visibly shaking. 'They have taken my roots away. That's my house. It didn't matter whether I visited Alderley Edge again as long as that house stayed there but the bastards have taken the floor away from under me.' Later he returns and is allowed to remove a souvenir, the corner post from the room where his father and grandfather were born, which was also where they died.

In 2017, when I told my brother about the demolition of Edge Croft, he made a long drive there on a Sunday when the site was quiet. The house had gone, but the builders had not yet started the massive removal of our ground. He took two hunks of masonry, one for each of us. He found the round stone balls that used to sit on top of the gateposts. One of these rolled off in 1967 and trundled several miles down the hill into the village, creating a hilarious caper-type chase that passed into family legend. The stone balls were too big to move without a crane or he would have brought those as souvenirs. He sent me a picture of them, furred with moss and lichen, nestling in the shrubbery. I guess they went in a skip with the rest of the spoil.

Alan, you got off lightly. You said they removed your floor. With Edge Croft, they didn't stop at the floor. They removed until they beheaded the whole hill.

When my brother and I were kids, there was an argument we used to regularly have. Which of us most belonged in Edge Croft?

'I do,' he said, 'because I was born here.'

'I do,' I said. 'Because I'm older and I was already living here when you were born.'

In 2019, my brother found an entry in our father's diaries about a couple who called in on Edge Croft in 1973. Their grandparents, whose surname was Powell, built Edge Croft in 1909 and sold it in the 1930s. Then in 1967, these younger Powells were visiting old haunts and saw, to their amazement, the house their grandparents built was up for sale. This was fate. They raced to the estate agent.

'Sorry,' said the agent. 'It just sold yesterday.'

That was to us.

A day earlier. A day later. These places come to us from random alignments; right people, right time, lucky fit. We think they belong to us for always, even if we never go back. Then they vanish when we're not looking, or are lost forever to someone else, and part of us vanishes too.

The Dust Is Settling

It's Boxing Day a year after our moving adventures. Dave and I are walking home in rainy darkness, full of good cheer after dinner at a friend's house. Maybe it's now the day after Boxing Day, as we're past midnight.

We are still in London, still making our near-daily trek to countryside, but on this night the metropolis also has charm. At Christmas it empties. The hum of travelling traffic, passers-by, commuters, builders and school children disappears. The office blocks go dark and the whole city lets out a collective holiday unwinding.

When you visit friends, you notice the ease of getting to them. They remark on the ease of coming to you. It feels as if that's how it always should be. At one time many more of those friends lived in walkable distance. Now walking to a friend — especially a longtime friend — is a rare and treasured novelty.

The friends we have BoxingNighted with are Oliver, Caroline and their daughters. Dave wrote the Dragon Warriors books with Oliver about forty years ago. We have BoxingNighted with Oliver and Caroline for so long that the arrangement is as fixed as Christmas itself. A quick mention is all that's needed. 'Our place on Boxing Night?' 'Of course.'

It might not have been. At the end of last year, we were embroiled in the Windfall farce and Mick and Steph were baying for our house or our blood. Oliver and Caroline too were on a threshold, renting in Sussex to see if they preferred that and should move out of London. Like our situation, that didn't prove straightforward.

We did Boxing Night that year too, wondering where we'd all be next time round.

A year on, here we are, still able to stroll from ours to theirs, and they from theirs to ours, to mark another Boxing Night in fine style.

For a long time we have been between places, asking ourselves where we now belong. We've had adventures. (Our house has too.) But tonight as Dave and I walk in the rain through the slumbering streets, it is as if the only people who exist are the characters of our personal London. It is still here, the London we have made from long friendships. This quiet route where we notice the slightest change, which leads to this gate we're unlatching, and this door that receives our keys and this lock that turns with a sound that has never changed in thirty-one (and thirty-nine) years. We're back. We're home.

If you've enjoyed this book, would you consider leaving a review on line or tell your book club? It makes all the difference to independent authors who rely on word of mouth to get their work known. Thank you!

About the author

Roz Morris lives in London, at least for the moment. Her first books were written in secret as a ghostwriter, then she came into the daylight with her own fiction: *My Memories of a Future Life*, *Lifeform Three* (longlisted for the World Fantasy Award and a finalist in the People's Book Prize) and *Ever Rest* (a grand finalist in the Eric Hoffer Award). She has another volume of unadventures *Not Quite Lost: Travels Without A Sense of Direction*.

She is also an editor and writing coach, and the author of the acclaimed *Nail Your Novel* series.

Where to find Roz

Tweet/X her as @Roz_Morris
Email her
rozmorriswriter@gmail.com
Explore her website rozmorris.wordpress.com

If you'd like to hear about other books in progress and receive new pieces of life writing every month, sign up here for her newsletter
tinyurl.com/rozmorrismailinglist

Not Quite Lost: Travels Without
A Sense of Direction

'Delightful, amusing and often very moving'

In life there's the fast lane and the scenic route. Take your time and you might meet people whose stories are as gripping as those of any famous name.

Not Quite Lost celebrates the hidden dramas in the apparently ordinary. A childhood home with a giant star-gazing telescope on the horizon. A tour guide in Glastonbury who is having a real-life romance with a character from Arthurian legend. A unit on a suburban business park where people are preparing to deep-freeze each other when they die.

But even low-key travel has its hazards, and Roz nearly runs down several gentlemen from Porlock when her brakes fail. She takes her marriage vows in a language she doesn't speak, has a *Strictly*-style adventure as a flashmob dancer, and hears an unexpected message in an experiment in ESP. Wry, romantic, amused and wonder-struck, *Not Quite Lost* is an ode to the quiet places you never realised might tell you a tale.

'Move over, Bill Bryson'

books2read.com/nql

Ever Rest

'I almost regret this is not a true story, because I believed every word.'

Grand finalist in the Eric Hoffer Award

Twenty years ago, Hugo and Ash were on top of the world. As the rock band Ashbirds they were poised for superstardom. Then Ash went missing, lost in a mountaineering accident, and the lives of Hugo and everyone around him were changed forever. Irrepressible, infuriating, mesmerizing Ash left a hole they could never hope to fill.

Two decades on, Ash's fiancée Elza is still struggling to move on, her private grief outshone by the glare of publicity. The loss of such a rock icon is a worldwide tragedy. Hugo is now a recluse in Nepal. Robert, a session player, feels himself both blessed and cursed by his time with Ashbirds, unable to achieve recognition in his own right. While the Ashbirds legend burns brighter than ever, Elza, Hugo and Robert are as stranded as if they were the ones lost in the ice. How far must they go to come back to life?

'Beautifully written story of loss, grief, fame and acceptance in a unique setting.'

books2read.com/everrest

My Memories of a Future Life

'Taut plotting and sharp storytelling'

'Amusing, mysterious, surreal and intense'

If your life was another person's past, what echoes would you leave in their soul? Could they be the answers you need now?

It's a question Carol never expected to face. She's a gifted musician who needs nothing more than her piano. She certainly doesn't think she's ever lived before. But forced by injury to stop playing, she fears her life may be over. Enter her soulmate Andreq; healer, liar, fraud and loyal friend. Is he her future incarnation or a psychological figment? And can his story help her discover how to live now?

'Much more than a twist on the traditional reincarnation tale...'
'A stunning achievement... like Doris Lessing but much more readable'

books2read.com/futurelife

Lifeform Three

'Beautifully written; meaningful. Top-drawer storytelling in the tradition of Atwood and Bradbury'

'I really didn't want this book to end. It's that good'

Longlisted for the World Fantasy Award. Finalist in the People's Book Prize

Misty woods; abandoned towns; secrets in the landscape; a forbidden life by night; the scent of bygone days; a past that lies below the surface; and a door in a dream that seems to hold the answers.

Paftoo is a 'bod'; made to serve. He is a groundsman on the last remaining countryside estate, once known as Harkaway Hall — now a theme park.

Paftoo holds scattered memories of the old days, but they are regularly deleted to keep him productive. When he starts to have dreams of the Lost Lands' past and his cherished connection with Lifeform Three, Paftoo is propelled into a nightly battle to reclaim his memories, his former companions and his soul.

books2read.com/lifeform3

Nail Your Novel books for writers

*Nail Your Novel: Why Writers Abandon Books &
How You Can Draft, Fix & Finish With Confidence*
Everything you need to take you from first
inspiration to final manuscript. Also available in
workbook format.

*Nail Your Novel: Writing Characters
Who'll Keep Readers Captivated*
How to create characters your readers will take to
their hearts.

*Nail Your Novel: Writing Plots
With Drama, Depth and Heart*
What will your fascinating characters do and will it
be interesting? How to build a cracking plot.

nailyournovel.wordpress.com/nail-your-novel-books/

www.ingramcontent.com/pod-product-compliance
Lightning Source LLC
Chambersburg PA
CBHW011127070526
44584CB00028B/3802